An Architecture of the Mind

T0373546

An Architecture of the Mind proposes a mathematically logical and rigorous theory of lived experience, and a comprehensive and coherent theory of psychology. It is also remarkably simple. Building on the core proposition that the mind is a network structure, it proposes a theory of the psychological process as operating within and upon that structure, and a theory of behaviour as determined by that process.

The theory presents a view of the mind which reveals a new perspective on the process of reasoning in thinking and how it may coexist with processes more akin to simple rule-following and computation. It allows us to understand the impact of social factors on psychological processes by revealing their role in and influence on mental networks. It reveals the place of motivations in the psyche as complexes in mental networks from whence aesthetics, preference and value judgements arise and demonstrates their necessity for behaviour. This book is especially useful for the perspective it offers on behavioural change. It reveals the conditions under which traditional economic theories of incentives will be appropriate, and the conditions under which they will not be.

This book draws on psychology, social science, cultural science, neuroscience and economics to offer an interdisciplinary contribution which resists the tendency for disciplines to become over-specialised and fragmented. It represents an important work for anyone interested in the functioning of the human mind and the government of human behaviour.

Dr. Brendan Markey-Towler is a philosopher, psychological scientist and economist. He received his Doctor of Philosophy from the University of Queensland in 2017, having researched there under Professors John Foster and Peter Earl and at University College London under Professor Michelle Baddeley. He lives in Brisbane, Queensland with his family.

An Architecture of the Mind

A Psychological Foundation for the
Science of Everyday Life

Brendan Markey-Towler

Routledge
Taylor & Francis Group

LONDON AND NEW YORK

First published 2018 by Routledge

2 Park Square, Milton Park, Abingdon, Oxfordshire OX14 4RN

52 Vanderbilt Avenue, New York, NY 10017

Routledge is an imprint of the Taylor & Francis Group, an informa business

First issued in paperback 2020

British Library Cataloguing-in-Publication Data
A catalogue record for this book is available from the British Library

Library of Congress Cataloging-in-Publication Data
A catalog record for this book has been requested

ISBN: 978-1-138-54966-1 (hbk)
ISBN: 978-0-367-60718-0 (pbk)

Typeset in Times New Roman
by Apex CoVantage, LLC

For John, Peter and Michelle, whose vision this is
For Mum and Dad, who kept me alive to sketch it
For Lucy, who brought light when all else was dark

Contents

Figures

Glossary of mathematical symbols

Symbol	Translation
$A \Rightarrow B$	"A" implies "B", or, if "A" then "B"
$A \Leftarrow B$	"A" is implied by "B", or, "A" only if "B"
$A \Leftrightarrow B$	"A" if and only if "B", or "A" implies "B" and "B" implies "A"
$\{A\}$	The set "A"
$A \subset B$	"A" is a subset of "B"
$A^{\,B}$	"A" is a superset of "B", or, "A" contains "B"
$A \vee B$	"A" or "B"
$A \& B$	"A" and "B"
$A \cup B$	The combination, or union, of the sets "A" and "B"
$A \cap B$	The intersection of the sets "A" and "B"
$A \setminus B$	The set "A" excluding the elements "B"
$a \in A$	"a" is an element of "A"
$\{a_i\}_{i=\alpha}^{\Omega}$	The sequence of elements "a" from "α" to "Ω"
$\lvert\{A\}\rvert$	The number of elements in set "A"
$\emptyset$	Empty set
2^A	The set of subsets of "A"
$A\colon B$	"A" such that "B"
$\forall A$	For all "A"
$\exists A$	There exists "A"
$A \circ B$	"A" defined on "B"
$f\colon A \to B$	The function, or process "f" takes points in set "A" and transforms them into points in "B"
$a = f(b)$	"a" is a function of "b", "b" is transformed by the process "f" into "a"
$A \succeq B$	"A" is at least as preferable as "B"
$A \succ B$	"A" is more preferable than "B"
$A \sim B$	"A" is equally as preferable as "B"
$\neg A$	Not "A", the opposite of "A"
$/$	A diagonal strike through any symbol negates it, i.e. inserts "is not" or "does not" before it
$\frac{\partial A}{\partial B}$	The change in "A" for a change in "B"

Preface

This is an unusual book. It's in the style of a traditional academic book, but it is not quite in the style of a modern academic book. It is theoretical, but motivated by practicality. It is mathematically logical, but also hopes to speak to the general reader. So to orient you to this work then, it might be worth taking Simon Sinek's advice to start with why. Why was *An Architecture of the Mind: A Psychological Foundation for the Science of Everyday Life* written?

This book was written because I, like many, wanted to understand humans. I wanted to understand how we fit into the world and interact with it. I wanted such an understanding, but also one which was integrated, holistic and systematic. This book was written because I sought, to draw inspiration from Alfred Marshall (1890), a "Science of Everyday Life".

I wrote this book because I needed a theory of how we orient ourselves to, and act, within the world. And I needed one which was at once more simple, more coherent and more comprehensive while also rigorous and general than those which currently exist. I needed that because I needed a theory which I could apply to understand *any* human behaviour, *all* human behaviour. That was the purpose of this book, to propose such a theory. It was motivated deeply by practicality, a desire to develop a foundation upon which a Science of Everyday Life could rest.

The point of this work is therefore to propose a mathematically logical and rigorous theory of our lived experience of the world. The purpose of this book is to offer an integrated, holistic and systematic psychological foundation for the Science of Everyday Life. It seeks to help us understand ourselves, which must surely be the basis for our understanding of our interaction with others. The Science of Everyday Life has its roots in psychology, but it extends into social science, sociology, anthropology, cultural science, political science and economics. The present work therefore proposes a foundation for this science upon which a view of human interaction may be built.

The present work offers a theory of psychology at the level of lived experience, i.e. mental experience. It offers a theory of the mind. It draws on, acknowledges and builds by reference to brain science, although it does not offer a general theory of the brain.

That said, it does offer the hope of a more coherent link between psychological science and brain science. In this sense, the present work is seeking to reach out from the psychological sciences toward the neurobiological view of humanity offered by Sapolsky (2017). This book proposes, in a sense, a focal point for going between neurobiological science and the Science of Everyday Life (what we now call the social and psychological sciences) via the theory of lived experience proposed here.

This book is therefore very much a beginning, not an end. The present work focuses on developing a theory of the mind to study the manner in which psychology interacts with the world at large and our behaviour. Further steps, the foundations for which are laid here in this book, will be to extend further the understanding of human behaviour it offers, to extend our understanding of psychopathological states of neurosis and psychosis, and to apply the theory proposed here to understanding systems of human interaction in economy, polity and society. The Science of Everyday Life must be founded upon a theory of our lived experience, of psychology. But it contains much more than that.

An *apologia* is in order here for the style of this book. Clearly, as you will already have seen, it is not quite in the style of modern academic work. This book is the start point for a project which seeks to resist the tendency of academia to fragment into ever more specialised, ever more hair-splitting subdisciplines.

There will be, therefore, many scholars and studies not cited in this book. The purpose of it is not to provide a survey of all the fields it draws on, but instead to draw on existing *ideas* to propose a new one. The purpose of this book is not therefore to seek to unify psychology *per se*, but rather to propose as comprehensive as possible a theory of mind which might form the core of a Science of Everyday Life. It seeks to bring as much of our knowledge to bear as possible on understanding our lived experience, drawing on philosophy, psychology, neuroscience, economics and sociology in an attempt to connect theory with practice and practical matters. It is a deeply interdisciplinary work in that it does not seek merely to cross-fertilise fields, but in fact to merge them. It aims to provide a useful theory to form a useful basis for a useful Science.

This book is thus more in the style of traditional academic books, those writings of old where a thinker would disappear to read and think for a number of years before returning to write down and present to the public at large what they discovered. This is not so common anymore simply because that is not the nature of modern academia, in which one is expected to build up a substantial corpus in specialised technical journals over many years before perhaps publishing a synthesis as a "pop book". I'm very grateful to Routledge and especially Lucinda Knight for affording me this opportunity to write in the old style.

A final word of preface. This work is formal, logical, mathematical and rigorous in its approach to the mind and psychology. However, I have also written it in such a way that were one to simply eliminate the mathematical symbols, one would still find the book coherent and integral. For those not of a mathematical bent, I would suggest that you try to grasp the symbols as a language of expression, but if that becomes overly taxing to simply gloss over them. No equation or symbol is set down which does not have its content explained immediately before or after it in plain English. A glossary of mathematical symbols is provided also to aid the reader.

That's something of my *apologia* for this work. I've found it extremely useful for my understanding of humanity and our interaction. I hope you will too.

References

Marshall, A., 1890. *Principles of Economics*, 8th Edition. Macmillan, London.
Sapolsky, R., 2017. *Behave*. Penguin, London.

Acknowledgements

I suppose if this work were to "belong" to anyone, it would be Peter Earl, Michelle Baddeley and John Foster. They provided me with the intellectual impetus for it, they provided me the intellectual support for it, and they carried me when I felt I couldn't go on.

This work arises especially from the unique influence of Peter Earl, my former Doctoral adviser now colleague, and his concept of the mind as a network. I am only now beginning to recognise his true genius. He was a behavioural economist before it was fashionable and his realisation of the central importance of the concept of substitutability to psychological and social science must surely become one of the greatest contributions to knowledge. Without his never-ending patience with my arrogant youth I would never have come to realise but a fraction of the profound knowledge he was trying to introduce me to.

Michelle Baddeley is the reason for this book. While studying with her at University College London, she set me upon the journey to writing this book with two fateful sentences, "you need to take more pity on your reader", and seven more "there's not much behavioural economics in your work just yet". She was referring to my Doctoral thesis, which was sprawling, complex and disorganised because the psychological theory at its core was not developed as coherently and fully as it ought to have been. Solving that problem is what led to the writing of this book, and it was her encouragement to finally and definitely grasp the nettle of psychology and behavioural economics forthrightly which brought this work into being.

John Foster, my great mentor, gave me my life's purpose as a third-year undergraduate, encouraged and nurtured my intellect, and carried me when I couldn't walk. I can't ever hope to repay him for the times he's hauled me out of the gutter where I've collapsed and set me on my feet to keep on the path toward knowledge. All my work is but an ongoing *Festschrift* to his legacy.

I would not dare to dedicate this book to him, and he will balk at his mention, but I cannot in good conscience fail to acknowledge the influence of Patrick Richards. His impact on my intellect has been nothing short of profound. I can only say that his *corpus* of teachings and writings represent nothing less than one of the greatest works of psychology in history.

For significant intellectual support I must give thanks to Enrico Petracca, one of the first to believe that my work might contain some idea of value. Roberto Scazzieri who put us in contact was thus indispensable for this work. Effie Konstantinou and D'Maris Coffman were responsible for bringing to my attention two of the most important books I've ever read, Margaret Archer's *Structure, Agency and the Internal Conversation*, and Michel de Certeau's *Practice of Everyday Life*, respectively. Without Sheri Markose I would never have looked so deeply into the profundities of Kurt Godel. Geoff Harcourt, the archetypal grandfather figure, provided the critical encouragement at the right time to continue this project. Louise West and Cerian Stanfield can never be repaid for their kindness in supporting me toward the conclusion of this project. Michael Knox must be accorded special thanks not only for introducing me to the Classics proper, but also for teaching me how to approach life and learning with a spirit of lightness and fun.

Lucinda Knight I've mentioned above, but she again deserves especial thanks for taking a risk and giving me the opportunity to publish here. She has a difficult job, all the more so for it having been such a big year for her on multiple fronts. But the massive relief she brought me when she offered me my contract I hope can serve as some recompense for her hard work.

Finally, a man cannot go through life without the support of his family. Mine are especially long suffering on my account and there are simply no words to even describe the debt I owe them for standing by me. For their keeping me alive in the dark times, always providing a haven to return to when it all became a bit too much and nurturing the fire within me in the midst of the storm, Mum and Dad can't but have this book dedicated to them alongside its intellectual parents. In keeping with her name, Lucy rolled back the darkness and brought the light. She believed in me and my work, she got me to see its strengths and potential. She read it from beginning to end to make sure it could be understood by someone other than myself. She brings the light to my life, I intend for her to bring it now and forever, and if I can bring but a fraction of that light to hers my life will have been well lived.

1 A fundamental question

What is the mind, how does it function?

There are two questions of philosophy and of science together that are arguably the greatest of all. The first is: what are the fundamental substances of physical reality, and the laws governing them and their interaction? The second question is: what is the mind, and how does it interact with the world? The first inquires about our external reality, and we have been remarkably successful in moving toward answering it. For the second, we look into our internal reality, and the present work aims to contribute toward its answering.

This book proposes a theory of the mind which is developed from the proposition that the mind is a network structure within which and upon which the psychological process operates. It utilises the mathematics of graph theory, or more colloquially, the mathematics of networks (Newman, 2003; Chartrand, 1985) to propose the existence of a structure which underlies the otherwise unfathomably complex and individuated phenomena of mental processes. Therefore this work proposes an "architecture" guiding the mental processes of perception, analysis and decision which evolves over time. This architecture reconciles many theories of psychology, indeed, perhaps all of those that currently exist. It also explains and predicts a number of psychological and behavioural phenomena observed by psychologists, neuroscientists, sociologists and economists.

First, we will consider some important philosophical questions concerning the nature of the mind. After taking a stance on these we shall introduce the concept of the mind as a network structure within which and upon which the psychological process operates. We will then use this concept as an architecture within which the psychology of behaviour exists and develop a theory of the process of perception, analysis, decision and the evolution of the mind over time. Naturally, not only a theory of behaviour, a theory of decision, but also a theory of *indecision*, of *inaction*, emerges from this.

The rest of this work will be occupied by efforts to elaborate how this theory explains various phenomena of psychology and behaviour within the context of a single, coherent theory, while reconciling many theories of the same by so doing. First we will consider how the psychological process may be interpreted as a process of reasoning or a process of rule-following, and by this duality arrive at the concept of dual-process psychology. In this chapter of interpretation we will also consider the place of the hypotheses of motivational theory as the basis of decision-making in both psychoanalytic and cognitive theories of psychology. We will also consider the manner in which social influences enter the psychological process. This in hand, we will turn to consider how various factors affect behaviour. First taking "quasi-fixed" environments, we discover the conditions under which traditional economic theories will be valid to be arbitrated by the existence of a state of substitutability. Then, in the final substantive chapter, we will consider the factors affecting behaviour in a more "wholesale" sense in which environments are free to vary and the whole psychological process affects behaviour in concert. This chapter will propose that there are a few core features of the architecture of mind reconciling the vast array of "heuristics and biases" identified in recent years and revealing them to be in fact the result of fundamental aspects of the human psyche long known to psychology, but hitherto somewhat disconnected.

This will form the core of our psychological foundation for the Science of Everyday Life. The conclusion of this work is not an end; it is a beginning in a long project to come to a new, useful Science of ourselves, our place in the world and our interaction with it. Proofs of theorems within this theory are relegated to the appendix as they are a matter of rigour primarily of interest to those of a technical persuasion, and detract from the development of the theory.

2 Philosophical considerations
The nature of the mind

To begin, we must take a stance on certain philosophical questions, ancient ones in point of fact. What is the mind and in what relation does it stand to the body and the world?

The first systematic treatment of these questions in Western philosophical tradition is given by Descartes (1637 & 1641). In an effort to purge his mind of any notions which might succumb to the sceptical, he found himself arriving at a fundamental truth which he found to be unshakable, related in a famous passage of his *Discourses*:

> But. . . I observed that, whilst I thus wished to think that all was false, it was absolutely necessary that I, who thus thought, should be somewhat; and as I observed that this truth, *cogito ergo sum*, was so certain of such evidence that no ground of doubt, however extravagant, could be alleged by the skeptics capable of shaking it, I concluded that I might, without scruple, accept it as the first principle of the philosophy of which I was in search.
>
> *Discourse IV*

We often translate *cogito ergo sum* as "I think therefore I am". But this is probably not quite faithful to Descartes' meaning. He probably would have said in the modern day something more like "I have cognition, I am aware, therefore I am". He had some faculty which allowed him to have the experience of existence, which allowed him to be *aware* of his existence. This was the mind.

He was also of the utterly unshakable belief that the external world existed, but independently of himself, for he perceived it yet was not consciously aware of creating it. To Descartes' thinking then there were two worlds; a "mental" world of ideas and contemplation where the mind was free to associate and generate ideas, and a physical world determined by the deterministic laws of nature. This is the "dualist" philosophy of mind, held to by many great minds of science and philosophy including (albeit with variations) David Chalmers (Chalmers, 1995, 1996), Sir John Eccles and Sir Karl Popper (Popper and Eccles, 1977) and Sir Roger Penrose (Penrose, 1989).

The present work, however, holds to a monist perspective on reality (that there is one unitary reality) and so Descartes' philosophy must succumb to the critique of Gilbert Ryle. In the *Concept of Mind* (1949) he famously (and a little unfairly) dismissed dualism as a philosophy of the "ghost in the machine". It was founded, to his mind, on a category mistake concerning the concept of "existence". Existence is a monist concept: there is only one unitary existence (Ryle, 1949, p.24). One reality, not two, for mind and world are clearly deeply connected and interact, even in Descartes' estimation.

Ryle did hold, however, that we have a mind. We do have a consciousness of our existence in the world and experience of it. He even rendered Descartes' description of this into a plainer English: the mind is that faculty by which we may "know what we are about" (Ryle, 1949, p.154). Thomas Nagel developed this notion in a famous paper (1974) titled "What Is it Like to Be a Bat?" Our mind is that in which exists "intentional states" (think *intensio* rather than "intent"), our awareness of our existence within and experience of the world.

But defining the mind we must not exclude the possibility of the subconscious or even the unconscious first explored (in Western tradition) by Sigmund Freud and Carl Jung. We know that we have such experiences as exist in the subconscious/unconscious mind for we feel their impact consciously whenever we have some feeling or emotion for which we cannot identify the cause (Freud, 1917, 1930, 1963; Jung, 1933, 1935, 1964). So we must allow that the mind and consciousness are not necessarily equivalent.

The mind is that element of our being which experiences our place in and relation to the world. We are conscious when we are aware of our place in and relation to the world.

The mind, then, is that in which our lived experience of our existence in the world occurs. By world we are not enforcing a dualist ontology so that the world is only external to ourselves – we are part of the world, the world is internal to us as well as external. It is a part of our being – mind, brain and body united as one whole in a monist world (Bennett and Hacker, 2003; Bennett et al., 2007). We *are* conscious, and are aware of our existence, though not necessarily of its totality.

A new question arises at this point: in what relation does the mind stand to our world?

The extreme solution to this question was proposed by Ryle's student Daniel Dennett (1991, 1996), who equates mind and brain. The mind is in this view totally reducible to the brain. It is thus known as the "strong Artificial Intelligence" view, for a machine which replicated the brain would be held to have an artificial intelligence indistinguishable from the intelligence of a human being.

A potential problem with such a view is that it would appear to deny the existence of consciousness as we experience it. If the mind *is* the brain and consciousness is real there must be some point in the brain where conscious experience is played out as on a screen in a theatre – a "Cartesian theatre" if you will. Given what we know about brains we know this to be absurd, so consciousness as we know it cannot be real.

Searle (1997), drawing on his assessment of the flurry of works published around the time, proposed a weaker form of this hypothesis. It seems absurd to deny the reality of consciousness as we experience it – it *is* the very awareness of such thoughts! Yet it appears that the brain is necessary and sufficient for the mind. If the brain does not function, we die and appear to cease being aware of our existence and place within the world. If the brain functions, we are alive. So the mind must in some sense be *emergent* from the brain.

Now if the mind is emergent from the brain, we might expect it to function in a similar fashion to the brain. The brain seems to have sufficient regularity for it to be capable of being modelled mathematically (Kandel et al., 2013, Appendices E,F). So we might expect the mind to be similarly amenable to being modelled mathematically. Indeed, we might be able to replicate the function of the mind in the working of a computer and thus create an Artificial Intelligence. Certainly, Turing (1950), von Neumann (1958), Newell et al. (1958, 1962), Simon (1969, 1991) and Samuel (1953, 1959) seem to have some success in that regard. Searle's philosophy thus justifies the basis for this work – we hold the mind under this philosophy to be an entity with regularity sufficient for us to theorise and represent mathematically.

Searle's philosophy, however, is one of "weak Artificial Intelligence". A machine constructed to replicate the function of a human mind is not necessarily the same as a human being in the particular of consciousness. Unless the machine is aware of its place in and relation to the world it is not equivalent with a human being. Searle puts it neatly when he makes a distinction between the "syntax" of mental processes and the "semantics" endowed them by consciousness. A machine may faithfully enough replicate the "syntax" of observing van Gogh's *Starry Night*, indeed one might argue that a camera does this. But not until it is *aware* of that experience and can *feel* the ecstatic beauty and chaotic glory of the cosmos swirling above us can we say that machine equals mind (cf. Jefferson, 1949, p.1110).

There is some consonance between the "weak Artificial Intelligence" philosophy and what we might (riskily) call "mystic" philosophies of the mind which draw heavily on Eastern traditions. No less an authority than Erwin Schrödinger (1944) turned to the great religious mystics surveyed by Huxley (1945) when faced by the gap between "life", "mind" and his famous "aperiodic crystal" (later known as DNA). These hold that there exists a field of consciousness pervading all of reality from whence ours arises at birth and to which it returns at death. They call this field the "Godhead".

We might hypothesise that such a field does exist, and that it is "concentrated" by the human brain into such a quanta as is sufficient for the human mind to exist. Such a process would make the brain both necessary and sufficient for the mind as in the weak Artificial Intelligence philosophy. It is also an idea not inconsistent with the thought of Thomas Nagel (2012) who has hypothesised there must be some as-yet undiscovered field pervading reality from which our consciousness derives. Daniel Siegel (2016) reaches a similar conclusion, hypothesising that the mind is an emergent, self-organising complex system regulating the flow of energy (the dual of information) across its field in reality – a theory which we will see is also consistent with our specific theory of the psychological process.

We hold to, or rather draw upon the philosophy of weak Artificial Intelligence and the mystic philosophy as regards the relation of mind (thus consciousness) to the brain, body and world. The mind is held to be emergent from the brain which is necessary and sufficient for it to exist, and mind, brain and body together constitute an individual's being in a monist world.

2.1   The form of mental processes: thought, language, the *gestalt* architecture of mind

What then, is the logico-mathematical form which can represent the function of the mind? Let us discover this by considering the most basic mental process: a thought. What is the nature of a thought?

We can find an unusual degree of agreement between philosophers and psychologists that the basic nature of thought is to form a *connection*. David Hume (1777) and Immanuel Kant (1781) both speak of thought as "connection" between objects and events in the world. Both Freud (1917, 1930, 1963) and Jung (1933, 1935, 1964) spoke of them as "association" of objects and events in the world – especially within ourselves. John Dewey (1910) spoke of thought as "inferring the unseen relations" between objects and events in our environment. George Kelly (1963) spoke of thoughts as "channelised" by the way in which we "construe events" in our personal constructs of the world. Herbert Simon (1947, 1956, 1959, 1967, 1969, 1976, 1978a,b) saw thought as a process of implementing various steps in behavioural rules, or algorithms, connecting each step to the next in the sequence. Friedrich Hayek (1952) saw thought as successive "classifications" of objects and events relative to higher and higher order conceptualisations of them. Kenneth Boulding (1961) spoke of thought as "filtered" through our "image" of the world. And we know that our brains, from which we hold the mind to emerge, are network structures consisting of synaptic connections between neural cells (Kandel et al., 2013; Sapolsky, 2017).

A mathematical formalism which permits us to represent the form of thoughts thus conceived as relational, connective, objects is graph theory, or more colloquially, the mathematics of networks. The basic mental process, a thought, is to express in language a relation $R_{hh'}$, or a connection, between two elements h, h'.

The mind is the totality of the manner in which an individual thinks about the world and infers the relation of the objects and events contained therein together. It is, to use an old nomenclature, a *gestalt*, a whole of organised (i.e. related) parts, a structure, an architecture of thought, the syntax, the linguistic expression of which we can represent using a graph, or more colloquially, a network.

Definition 1 (The mind). The mind of the individual is a network system, or *gestalt*

$$\mu = \{H \quad g(H)\} \tag{2.1}$$

consisting of elements $h \in H$ representing the *objects and events of reality* related to one another by relations $R_{hh'} \in g(H)$ between the objects and events of reality h, $h' \in H$ within a graph, or network.

The Germans would call this mental network our *Weltanschauung*, our "worldview". Karl Polanyi (1958) would have said it expresses our "personal knowledge" of how the objects and events in our world relate to one another. Hayek (1952) would have called it our "map" of reality and Boulding (1961) our "image" of the world. Kelly (1963) would have called it our system of personal constructions of reality, our personality.

However we interpret it, the mental network μ expresses the individual's understanding of the objects and events in their world and expresses it in a *language*. This language is not necessarily equivalent to any spoken language, it may be "pictoral" or "symbolic" *a la* the philosophy of Ludwig Wittgenstein (Wittgenstein, 1914–1916, 1921; Wittgenstein et al.,

1930–1932; Wittgenstein, 1953). It might even be inexpressible but as symbols (Jung, 1964) or even extant within the "tacit dimension" of which we cannot actually speak (Polanyi, 1967). Nevertheless, the elements of that language H are the equivalents of nouns, adjectives, subjects, objects. The connectives of that language are the equivalents of verbs, adverbs, propositions, conjunctions. It provides the manner of expression for the "syntax" of thought which the consciousness endows semantics (meaning) to (Searle, 1997).

2.2   The evolution of the mind: consciousness, creativity, psychological indeterminacy

If consciousness is accepted as real, it seems reasonable that one would allow for an *active* consciousness, for us to be aware of the experience of thinking *and* to engage in that experience. If we didn't allow for engaged and active thought in consciousness, then consciousness would seem to be a passive "ghost in the machine" sort of consciousness. Siegel (2016) would appear to be in agreement with this notion insofar as he sees the mind as a conscious regulator of energy and information flow. But if we allow consciousness to be real in this manner, we allow the possibility of thoughts which exist for no reason other than "we" (the phenomenological "I" (Luijpen, 1969)) think them consciously and actively. The existence of such a thought does not itself break the principle of sufficient reason (Melamed and Lin, 2015), but the "I" thinking them might. That the "I" brings into being a conscious thought might be the terminus of a particular chain of causation.

We call such thoughts to exist "genuinely creative thought", they are thoughts which exist for no reason other than they are created by the phenomenological "I". The capability to imagine new things is endowed by the conscious mind. This poses a difficulty for mathematical models which by their nature (consisting always of statements $A \Rightarrow B$) require the principle of sufficient reason to hold. Active conscious thought, insofar as it may be genuinely creative is indeterminate until it exists. However, that we might not be able to determine the existence of such thoughts before they are extant does not preclude us from representing them once their existence is determined. Koestler (1964) taught that all acts of creation are ultimately acts of "bisociation", that is, of linking two things together in a manner hitherto not the case. Acts of creation, bisociations made by the conscious mind, are indeterminate before they exist, but once they exist they can be represented as relations $R_{hh'}$ between two objects of reality h, h'. We may think of such acts of creation as akin to the *a priori* synthetic statements of which Kant (1781) spoke.

This is no matter of mere assertion. Roger Penrose (1989) holds, and it is difficult to dismiss him, that the famous theorems of Kurt Godel imply something unique exists in the human consciousness. The human mind can "do" something no machine can. Godel demonstrated that within certain logical systems there would be true statements which could not be so verified within the confines of the logical system but would require verification by the human consciousness. The consciousness realises connections – in this case truth-values – which cannot be realised by the machinations of mathematical logic alone. It *creates*. The human mind can therefore (since we have seen those connections made) create connections in the creation of mathematical systems irreducible to machination alone. There are certain connections which consciousness alone can make.

The problem of conscious thought goes a little further though. New relations may be presented to the consciousness either by genuinely creative thought or otherwise, but they must be actually incorporated into the mind, $R_{hh'} \in g(H) \subset \mu$ and take their place alongside others in the totality of thought $g(H) \subset \mu$. Being a matter of conscious thought by the phenomenological "I", the acceptance or rejection of such relations is something we cannot determine until the "I" has determined the matter. As Cardinal Newman demonstrated in his *Grammar of Assent* (1870), connections may be presented to the phenomenological "I", but they are merely presented to the "I" and therefore inert until the "I" *assents* to them – accepts and incorporates them into that individual's worldview. The question of assent to various connections presented to the "I" is an either/or question Newman recognises is ultimately free of the delimitations of reason and a matter for resolution by the "I" alone.

There are thus two indeterminacies introduced to any psychological theory by the existence of consciousness:

1   Indeterminacy born of the possibility of imagining new relations $R_{hh'}$ in genuinely creative thought.
2   Indeterminacy born of the acceptance or rejection by conscious thought of any new relation $R_{hh'}$ and their incorporation or not into the mind $\mu \supset g(H)$.

The reality of consciousness thus places a natural limit on the degree to which we can determine the processes of the mind, determine those thoughts which will exist prior to their existence. For psychology, this indeterminacy of future thought until its passage and observance is the (rough) equivalent of the indeterminacy introduced to the physical world by Heisenberg's principle, the principle underlying the concept of the "wave function" upon which an indeterminate quantum mechanics operates (under certain interpretations (Kent, 2012; Popper, 1934, Ch.9)).

2.3   Philosophical conclusions

We hold to the following philosophical notions in this work. The mind is that element of our being which experiences our place in the world and relation to it. We are conscious when we are aware of our place in and relation to the world. We hold to a mix of the "weak Artificial Intelligence" and mystic philosophies that mind is emergent from the brain and that mind, brain and body constitute the individual existing in a monist reality. The mind is a network structure $\mu = \{H \quad g(H)\}$ expressing the connections $g(H)$ the individual construes between the objects and events in the world H, an architecture within which and upon which the psychological process operates. The reality of consciousness introduces an indeterminacy into that architecture which imposes a limit on our ability to determine the psychological process.

References

Bennett, M., Dennett, D., Hacker, P., Robinson, D., Searle, J., 2007. *Neuroscience and Philosophy*. Columbia University Press, New York.

Bennett, M., Hacker, P., 2003. *The Philosophical Foundations of Neuroscience*. Blackwell, Oxford.

Boulding, K., 1961. *The Image*. University of Michigan Press, Ann Arbor.

Chalmers, D., 1995. Facing up to the problem of consciousness. *Journal of Consciousness Studies* 2 (3), 200–219.

Chalmers, D., 1996. *The Conscious Mind*. Oxford University Press, Oxford.

Chartrand, G., 1985. *Introductory Graph Theory*. Dover, Mineola.

Dennett, D., 1991. *Consciousness Explained*. Little, Brown, New York.

Dennett, D., 1996. *Kinds of Minds*. Phoenix, London.

Descartes, R., 1637 & 1641. *Discourse on Method and the Meditations*. Penguin, London.

Dewey, J., 1910. *How We Think*. D.C. Heath and Co., Lexington.

Freud, S., 1917. *A General Introduction to Psychoanalysis*. Wordsworth Editions, Hertfordshire.

Freud, S., 1930. *Civilisation and Its Discontents*. Penguin, London.

Freud, S., 1963. *Therapy and Technique*. Collier, New York.

Hayek, F., 1952. *The Sensory Order*. University of Chicago Press, Chicago.

Hume, D., 1777. *An Enquiry Concerning Human Understanding*, 2nd Edition. Hackett Publishing Company, Cambridge.

Huxley, A., 1945. *The Perennial Philosophy*. Chatto and Windus, London.

Jefferson, G., 1949. The mind of mechanical man. *British Medical Journal* 1 (4616), 1105–1110.

Jung, C., 1933. *Modern Man in Search of a Soul*. Routledge, London.

Jung, C., 1935. *Analytical Psychology*. Routledge, London.

Jung, C. (Ed.), 1964. *Man and His Symbols*. Bantam Doubleday Dell, New York.

Kandel, E., Schwartz, J., Jessell, T., Siegelbaum, S., Hudspeth, A. (Eds.), 2013. *Principles of Neural Science*, 5th Edition. McGraw-Hill, New York.

Kant, I., 1781. *Critique of Pure Reason*. Penguin, London.

Kelly, G., 1963. *A Theory of Personality*. Norton, New York.

Kent, A., 2012. Real world interpretations of quantum theory. *Foundations of Physics* 42, 421–435.

Koestler, A., 1964. *The Act of Creation*. Pan Books Ltd, London.

Luijpen, W., 1969. *Existential Phenomenology*. Literary Licensing, Inc., Whitefish.

Melamed, Y., Lin, M., 2015. Principle of sufficient reason. In: Zalta, E. (Ed.), *The Stanford Encyclopedia of Philosophy*, Spring 2015 Edition. Stanford University, Stanford.

Nagel, T., 1974. What is it like to be a bat? *Philosophical Review* 83 (4), 435–450.

Nagel, T., 2012. *Mind and Cosmos*. Oxford University Press, Oxford.

Newell, A., Shaw, J., Simon, H., 1958. Elements of a theory of human problem solving. *Psychological Review* 65 (3), 151–166.

Newell, A., Shaw, J., Simon, H., 1962. Contemporary Approaches to Creative Thinking. Behavioral Science Series. Atherton Press, New York, Ch. The processes of creative thinking, pp. 63–119.

Newman, J., 1870. *An Essay in Aid of a Grammar of Assent*. Oxford University Press, Oxford.

Newman, M., 2003. The structure and function of complex networks. *SIAM Review* 45 (2), 167–256.

Penrose, R., 1989. *The Emperor's New Mind*. Oxford University Press, Oxford.

Polanyi, M., 1958. *Personal Knowledge*. Routledge and Kegan Paul, London.

Polanyi, M., 1967. *The Tacit Dimension*. Routledge and Kegan Paul, London.

Popper, K., 1934. *Logic of Scientific Discovery*. Routledge, London.

Popper, K., Eccles, J., 1977. *The Self and Its Brain*. Springer, Heidelberg.

Ryle, G., 1949. *The Concept of Mind*. Penguin, London.

Samuel, A., 1953. Computing bit by bit, or, digital computers made easy. *Proceedings of the I.R.E.* 41 (10), 1223–1230.

Samuel, A., 1959. Some studies in machine learning using the game of checkers. *IBM Journal of Research and Development* 3 (3), 210–229.

Sapolsky, R., 2017. *Behave*. Penguin, London.

Schrödinger, E., 1944. *What Is Life?* Cambridge University Press, Cambridge.

Searle, J., 1997. *The Mystery of Consciousness*. New York Review of Books, New York.

Siegel, D., 2016. *Mind*. W.W. Norton, New York.

Simon, H., 1947. *Administrative Behavior*, 4th Edition. The Free Press, New York.

Simon, H., 1956. Rational choice and the structure of the environment. *Psychological Review* 63 (2), 129–138.

Simon, H., 1959. Theories of decision-making in economics and behavioural science. *American Economic Review* 49 (3), 3.

Simon, H., 1967. Motivation and emotional controls of cognition. *Psychological Review* 74 (1), 29–39.

Simon, H., 1969. *The Sciences of the Artificial*. MIT Press, Cambridge, MA.

Simon, H., 1976. *Method and Appraisal in Economics*. Cambridge University Press, Cambridge, Ch. From substantive to procedural rationality, pp. 129–148.

Simon, H., 1978a. On how to decide what to do. *Bell Journal of Economics* 9 (2), 494–507.

Simon, H., 1978b. Rationality as a process and as product of thought. *American Economic Review* 68 (2), 1–16.

Simon, H., 1991. Organizations and markets. *Journal of Economic Perspectives* 5 (2), 25–44.

Turing, A., 1950. Computing machinery and intelligence. *Mind* LIX (236), 433–460.

von Neumann, J., 1958. *The Computer and the Brain.* Yale University Press, New Haven.

Wittgenstein, L., 1914–1916. *Notebooks, 1914–1916,* 2nd Edition. University of Chicago Press, Chicago.

Wittgenstein, L., 1921. *Tractatus Logico-Philosophicus.* Routledge, London.

Wittgenstein, L., 1953. *Philosophical Investigations*, 4th Edition. Wiley-Blackwell, Chichester.

Wittgenstein, L., King, J., Lee, D., 1930–1932. *Wittgenstein's Lectures: Cambridge 1930–1932.* Rowman & Littlefield, Lanham.

3 The psychology of behaviour
Operating within and upon the architecture of mind

An individual exists within the world. They are influenced by and interact with that system. The world-system may be conceived of as containing information which we may represent as subsets of an arbitrary semiotic space. By information we mean pre-sensory information in the information-theoretic sense (Shannon, 1948a,b) employed in physical science.

Definition 2 (The world as information). The world contains a particular realisation, $v \subset V$, of all possible information contained within the world, V.

This is a formalism of the initial proposition of Wittgenstein (1921) that the world, all that is the case, is the totality of facts. Here facts, what is the case, are represented by information v. The whole information of the world however is not available to the individual, for the individual exists at a particular location within the world system.

Definition 3 (The individual's neighbourhood). The individual occupies a particular neighbourhood N within the world system.

We shall leave the notion of "neighbourhood" within the world-system formally undefined but for the usual connotations attached to the notion of "neighbourhood" and that it must account for the orientation of the sensory organs in physical space, not being merely a mathematical "ball" in physical space. For instance, when placing the individual within the context of a network, their neighbourhood N includes a set of other individuals the individual is directly connected to. We can now define the information contained within the neighbourhood of the individual within the world-system.

Definition 4 (The individual's environment). The individual's environment contains the information $v_N \subset v$ associated with their neighbourhood N

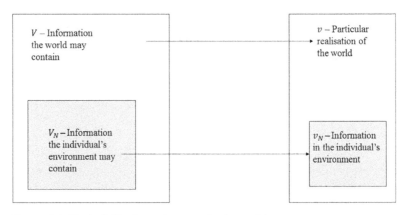

Figure 3.1 The individual's environment in the world.

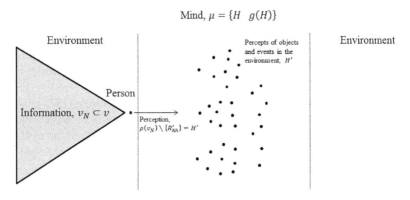

Figure 3.2 Perception, ρ (v_N) of a particular environment v_N by the individual.

within the world, which is a subset $v_N \subset V_N$ of all possible information which may be contained within their neighbourhood $V_N \subset V$.

The information contained within an individual's environment is not to be conceived of as exclusively that within their external environment (external to their bodies). Following Simon (1956), the information contained within their neighbourhood in the world-system is to be conceived of as *both* that contained within their external environment and that contained within their internal environment (within their bodies). Any information which makes an impression on the sensory organs and the nervous system is part of v_N.

The theory of psychology and behaviour to be now developed operates on the individual's locality within the world-system and the information contained therein. It shall consist of three consecutive stages. The individual first perceives their particular environment in the world, then they form an understanding of that particular environment by applying their mental networks either consciously or subconsciously, and make decisions to act on the basis of the understanding thus arrived at. Psychological science thus studies that which operates on and influences that with which physical science is concerned.

3.1 Perception

The information v_N contained within the environment of the individual must be transformed into representations of the objects and events therein contained within their mind before their psychology may operate on it. This is the function of perception, which maps information contained in the individual's environment into representations of that information in the mind. To put it in the manner Merleau-Ponty (1945, 1948) might have, perception provides the interface between the world and our personal knowledge of it (Polanyi, 1958), our personal experience of it.

Definition 5 (Perception). Perception maps subsets $v_N \subset V_N$ of information V_N contained within the neighbourhood N of the individual (their environment) into subsets $H' \subset H$ of a set of symbolic representations, or *percepts*, of the objects of reality, H, and any apparent relations between them R

$$\rho : 2^{V_N} \rightarrow 2^H \cup 2^R \tag{3.1}$$

so that upon the realisation of the world $v \in V$ the individual perceives $\rho(v_N) = \{H' \quad \{R_{hh'}\}\}$ the information $v_N \subset V_N$ contained within their environment as a set of percepts of the objects of reality, $H' \subset H$, and any apparent relations between them $\{R_{hh'}\} \subset R$. An individual may perceive an apparent relation $R_{hh'}$ between objects of reality only if they perceive those objects of reality, that is $R_{hh'} \in \rho(v_N) \Rightarrow h,h' \in \rho(v_N)$.

This mapping is the mental equivalent of the concept of the "perceptron" mapping in neuroscience (Kandel et al., 2013, Appendix E, F) which theorises the process whereby where electrical signals from the sensory organs are filtered through synaptic networks to neuron clusters encoding the basis for their representation in the mind. It emerges from the operation of the brain upon the sensory data gathered from the interaction of the body with the world (Mastrogiorgio and Petracca, 2016).

Figure 3.3 Shifting perceptions of information in a context: the vase and the faces.

Each percept $h \in H'$ either constitutes a symbolic representation of an object or event contained within the particular environment v_N, or an attribute of such an object or event (themselves objects and events). They are "pictures" or "words" corresponding to the objects and events in our world; potential actions, physical objects, things which might describe them, and feelings.

This representation is never "objective" in the classical sense of that word, it is at best "positionally" objective as described by Amartya Sen (1993), which is to say that the information they perceive is contingent upon their neighbourhood N, which affects the information $v_N \subset v$ available to them. Perception of any particular information $v' \subset v_N$ *contained within* a particular environment v_N cannot be spoken of in isolation; we must speak of perception of that particular information *contained within* perception of a particular environment $\rho\ (v_N)$.

The perception of the same information $v' \subset v'_{N'}$ in a different neighbourhood N' and therefore a different environment $v'_{N'}$ is not necessarily the same as perception in the environment N and context v_N. The famous "duckrabbit" example of the later work of Wittgenstein (1953) demonstrates this contingency of perception – the changing "pictures" of information in a particular environment – quite nicely, as do a number of other polymorphous pictures. Simply by varying the viewpoint, for instance, by the direction of the eye's glance (changing neighbourhood N), or shifting the image from landscape to portrait or being told to look for a certain image (changing v_N) can change the representation of information contained in a particular environment.

We will have more to say about the exact properties of the perception mapping $\rho\ (\cdot)$ in chapter 6, for instance how it is not divorced from the structure of mental networks. It suffices however for now to say that an individual's perception ρ ($v' \subset v_N$) of any particular information $v' \subset v_N$ contained within a particular environment $v_N \subset v$ must exist within the intersection of percepts of that information ρ (v') and percepts of the particular environment ρ (v_N) in which that information is contained.

Definition 6 (Perception of information contained in a particular environment). Percepts ρ ($v' \subset v_N$) of a particular subset $v' \subset v_N$ of information contained within a particular environment v_N, are the percepts contained within the intersection of percepts of that information alone ρ (v') and percepts of information contained within a particular environment ρ (v_N).

$$\rho\left(v' \subset v_N\right) = \rho(v') \cap \rho\left(v_N\right) \qquad (3.2)$$

An individual may perceive within a subset $v' \subset v_N$ of information contained within a particular environment v_N an apparent relation $R_{hh'}$ between objects of reality only if they perceive those objects of reality, that is $R_{hh'} \in \rho$ ($v' \subset v_N$) $\Rightarrow$ $h, h' \in \rho$ ($v' \subset v_N$).

In this manner we recognise the contingency, the context-dependence, of perception on the environment and neighbourhood of the individual. Individuals never perceive exactly what exists, they must at least perceive from a particular position in which only certain viewpoints on information can be obtained.

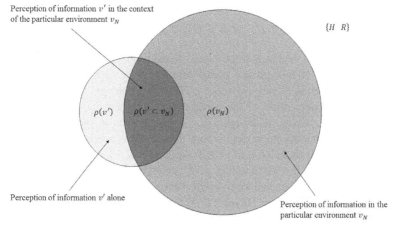

Figure 3.4 Perception of information $v' \subset v_N$ in the context of the particular environment v_N.

3.2   Analysis

For a particular environment v_N now we have a set of percepts $\rho\ (v_N) =$ $\{H'\ \{R_{hh'}\}\}$ of the objects and events H' and apparent relations between them $R_{hh'}$. Perception presents a "picture" of their environment to the individual (Merleau-Ponty, 1945, 1948). They have (literally) a view of their environment, external and internal. But this is not the same as understanding it – being able to construe the relations and connections of the various objects and events contained within their environment. Percepts have little meaning until we relate them together, and form an understanding exactly of how they relate to each other. This understanding is formed by applying the totality of thoughts an individual has in their mind, their mental networks, specifically the relations $g(H)$ construed between the objects of reality (definition 1). This we call the process of analysis. The process of analysis is the process of thinking about the perceived environment, and construing the relation of percepts of objects and events $H' \subset H$ contained therein based on personal knowledge of the world $g(H)$.

Definition 7 (Analysis, the process of thought). *Analysis, the process of thought, consists of connecting percepts $H' \subset \rho\ (v_N)$ of the objects and events in the individual's environment v_N based on their understanding of the relations $g(H)$ between percepts of the objects and events H contained within their mental networks $\mu = \{H\ g(H)\}$. From the process of analysis emerges an individual's understanding of their environment, which consists of the connections $g(H')$ they construe between the percepts $H' \subset \rho\ (v_N)$ of the objects and events within their environment v_N, that is*

$$g\left(H'\right) = \left\{R_{hh'} \in g(H) : h, h' \in H'\right\} \subset g\left(H\right) \qquad (3.3)$$

The definition of thought, the basic mental process, can now be refined in this context. A thought is a connection $R_{hh'} \in g(H')$ made by applying the connections in mental networks $g(H)$ to two percepts $h,\ h' \in H'$ contained within perception of the particular environment $v_N : \rho\ (v_N) \supset H'$. The neural correlates of thought, $R_{hh'} \in g(H')$, exist in the excitation of "associative memory networks" within the overall synaptic network structure of the brain (Kandel et al., 2013, Appendix E, F).

The notion that understanding $g(H')$ emerges from applying relations $g(H)$ construed in personal knowledge (Polanyi, 1958) of the world is consistent with Friedrich von Hayek's (1952) theory of psychology whereby a "model" of a particular environment, $g(H')$ emerges from progressive "classification" in thought guided by a semi-permanent "map" of reality $g(H)$. Likewise Boulding (1961) speaks of our "image" of reality $g(H)$

The psychology of behaviour 19

Mind, $\mu = \{H \quad g(H)\}$

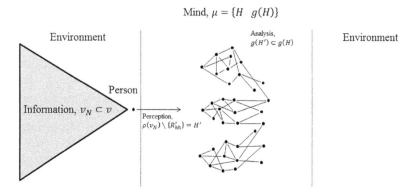

Figure 3.5 The process of analysis: the individual forms an understanding $g(H') \subset g(H)$ of the objects and events $H' \subset \rho (v_N)$ contained within their environment v_N.

(a German would say *Weltanschauung*) through which our perception of sensory data H' is filtered to arrive at understanding $g(H')$.

The interpretation George Kelly (1963) would offer of this process is particularly interesting. Kelly's fundamental postulate is that thoughts $R_{hh'} \in g(H')$ are "channelised" by the way in which we "construe events" in our system of personal constructs of reality $g(H)$. Our system of personal constructs $g(H)$ express the ways in which we construe events to occur, how they relate to one another. Insofar as they express the way we think about the world, our system of personal constructs expresses our *personality*. So, when we perceive a particular situation $\rho (v_N) \supset H'$, the understanding which emerges from our analysis $g(H') \subset g(H)$ is a reflection of our *personality*.

David Hume (1777, p.14) identifies three types of connection, or association which exist in the individual's understanding of the world $g(H)$ which become thoughts when applied to analysing, $g(H') \subset g(H)$, a particular environment $v_N : \rho (v_N) \supset H'$:

- **Resemblance**: An object h, say, a painting, *resembles* (is similar to, literally reminds us of) an object h', the person of whom h is a painting (Hume, 1777, pp.33–34). The relation of the two, $R_{hh'} \in g(H')$ indicates this resemblance. This link is almost certainly (though not necessarily) undirected, and the relation symmetric, $R_{hh'} = R_{h'h}$ so that the object h resembles the object h' and vice versa (son resembles father, father resembles son).
- **Contiguity**: An object h, say, my wife, is *contiguous*, exists in connection with another h', the concept of "woman" or "beauty", or even

more simply, her name (Hume, 1777, pp.34–35). $R_{hh'} \in g(H')$ represents this conjunction of the two objects. If this link is directed, $R_{hh'} \neq R_{h'h}$, the object h' is contiguous with, but stands in asymmetric relation to the other, h, in some manner ("my wife is a woman"). If this link is undirected, $R_{hh'} = R_{h'h}$, the object h is simply conjunctive with, exists in symmetric relation to and connection with the other, h', and vice versa ("my wife is A, A is my wife").

• **Cause and effect**: An event h, say, a billiard ball striking another is the *cause* of another event h', the other billiard ball moving, which is the *effect* of the event h (Hume, 1777, p.51). The link $R_{hh'} \in g(H')$ representing this relation, $h \Rightarrow h'$ is a directed link, non-symmetrical ($R_{hh'} \neq R_{h'h}$) representing the causal relationship construed between these two objects. Such a relation may contain one or both of two different forms: "I have found that such an object has always been attended with such an effect" in the past (Hume, 1777, p.22), and "I foresee, that other objects, which are, in appearance, similar, will be attended with similar effects" in the future (Hume, 1777, p.22).

Thoughts, especially of the final type, thus may be interpreted as expressions of expectation. Thoughts construe the manner in which events proceed (Kelly, 1963), and so the process of analysis may construe what events may be expected to succeed the present state of affairs in the future (Shackle, 1969, 1972; Taleb, 2007). From the question of how such thoughts might be justified emerged Hume's famous problem of inductive logic (Hume, 1777, p.22). For even if justified by a calculation of probability as the "limit proportion" within a population of events (the "frequentist" view (Popper, 1934, Ch.8)), the individual, in construing their expectations, betrays a belief that "radical" uncertainty (Shackle, 1969, 1972) will not throw up a wholly new category of event into reality – the categorical "Black Swan" event (Taleb, 2007). Ultimately our thought must be justified by none other than pure belief which may only ever be corroborated or falsified, never proven.

3.3 Decision

The outcome of the process of perception and analysis can at this stage be summarised by the object

$$g(H') = g(\rho(v_N)\backslash\{R_{hh'}\}) \subset g(H) \qquad (3.4)$$

which represents the understanding, the assessment $g(H')$ an individual has formed of the particular environment v_N they are in, their reaction to it based on their perception $\rho(v_N)\backslash\{R_{hh'}\}$ of the objects of reality in that particular environment, and their understanding $g(H)$ of the world How, now, does this provide the basis for decision, act, and behaviour?

The nature of acts and behaviour

The considerations of this section are technical and need not especially trouble the reader. They are provided largely for the sake of rigour and have little role in the theory as a whole. If an individual must act, their act will manifest in behaviour, which exists within the information contained within a particular environment.

Definition 8 (Behaviour). In any particular environment v_N, there is information $v_N^a \subset v_N$ corresponding to the individual's *potential* behaviour which is a strict subset of that particular environment (that is, $v_N^a \subset v_N$ but $v_N^a \not\supset v_N$). Within this is information $v_N^{a^*} \subset v_N^a \subset v_N$ which corresponds to the behaviour which is both potential and *realised* behaviour. The potential behaviour $v_N^a \subset v_N$ of the individual in a particular environment is contained within information $V_a \subset V$ corresponding to all potential behaviour, such that potential behaviour is at the intersect of this with the environment, $v_N^a = v_N \cap V_a$ (hence both $v_N^a \subset v_N$ and $v_N^a \subset V_a$).

Acts between which the individual must decide which correlate to this behaviour correspond to perceptions of this potential behaviour in the mind. But merely perceiving those bits of information and any apparent relations between them is not enough for them to constitute a potential course of action. Potential behaviour must exist within the individual's perception and understanding $\{H' \quad g(H')\}$ of that particular environment.

Definition 9 (Acts). Acts $a \subset A \subset \{H \quad g(H)\}$ are the correlates in the mind of the information corresponding to behaviour. In a particular environment v_N, the potential acts $a \subset A' \subset \{H' \quad g(H')\}$ of the individual which correlate to the potential behaviour $v_N^a \subset v_N$ are perceptions of that behaviour which exist within the mind.

$$A' = \rho\left(v_N^a \subset v_N\right) \cap \{H' \quad g(H')\} \subset A \qquad (3.5)$$

The set of potential behaviours $A \subset \{H \quad g(H)\}$ is a strict subset of the mind $\{H \quad g(H)\}$ (that is, $A \subset \{H \quad g(H)\}$ and $A \not\supset \{H \quad g(H)\}$), and any set of potential courses of action in a particular environment A' is included within it, that is, $A \supset A' \, \forall \, v_N^a$. The realised behaviour $v_N^{a^*}$ of the individual correlates in the mind with an intersect between a subset $\rho\left(v_N^{a^*}\right) \subset \rho\left(v_N^a \subset v_N\right)$ of perceptions of that behaviour with the set of potential behaviour in a particular environment, $a^* = \rho\left(v_N^{a^*}\right) \cap A' \subset A'$ which we

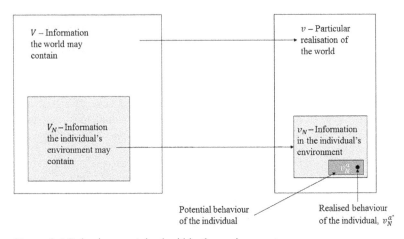

Figure 3.6 Behaviour contained within the environment v_N.

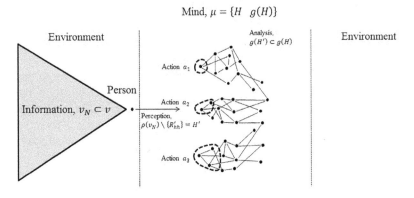

Figure 3.7 Identifying potential actions a_1, a_2, a_3.

call their realised course of action. If perception $\rho\left(v_N^{a^*}\right) \subset \rho\left(v_N^a \subset v_N\right)$ of the realised behaviour $v_N^{a^*}$ of the individual contains an apparent relation $R_{hh'}$ between objects of reality, it must also include those objects of reality, that is $R_{hh'} \in \rho\left(v_N^{a^*}\right) \Rightarrow h, h' \in \rho\left(v_N^{a^*}\right)$.

The reason perception of realised behaviour $\rho\left(v_N^{a^*}\right)$ is allowed to exist without caveat within the perceptions of potential behaviour within a particular environment $\rho\left(v_N^a \subset v_N\right)$ is that if the individual is to actually engage in the behaviour $v_N^{a^*}$ it stands to reason the perceptions of that behaviour must be included within the set of perceptions' potential behaviour.

Leaving the overall set of actions A vaguely defined as we have done does not particularly affect the results or interpretation of the present theory, and to define it would generate considerable complexity without much benefit. Where we do wish to speak of A in the sense of being the set of all behaviour of which the individual is aware, it is sufficient definition that we require A to include all sets of potential behaviours in particular environments A'.

Immediately with definition 9, we can demonstrate that an act must include within perception of behaviour percepts of the objects and events within the world, in other words, behaviour cannot be meaningfully perceived as their relation alone.[1]

Corollary 1 (Acts contain objects or events of reality). *An individual's realised course of action $a^* \subset A$ must, if it is non-empty ($a^* \neq \emptyset$), contain objects or events of reality, that is, $\exists h \in a^*$.*

We can demonstrate further that the sets of all possible actions A, and of potential actions in a particular environment A' must be nonempty if an individual is to act and that there must exist a behavioural mapping between the particular environment in which the individual finds themselves and their behaviour in that environment.

Theorem 1 (Existence of acts and behavioural mappings). *Suppose the individual cannot act in a particular environment v_N containing the realised behaviour $v_N^{a^*} \subset v_N^a \subset v_N$ within the set of potential behaviour $v_N^a \subset v_N$ without perception of it, that is, $\rho\left(v_N^{a^*}\right) = \emptyset \Rightarrow \nexists v_N^{a^*} \subset v_N$. If an individual is to act then*

1   *The sets of potential acts A' and all possible acts A must be non-empty, the intersect of all possible acts A with percepts of the objects and events of reality $A \cap H$ must be non-empty, that is $A \cap H \neq \emptyset$, and at least one act must exist within the objects of reality perceived in a particular situation H', that is $A \cap H' \neq \emptyset$.*

2   *A single valued mapping $d : V_N \rightarrow 2^A$ must exist assigning out of all information the behaviour of the individual, one course of action $a^* \in 2^A$. Only one subset of all possible courses of action A may be selected in any particular environment, that is, $a^* \in d(v_N) \Rightarrow a' \notin d(v_N) \forall a' \in A$.*

This single valued mapping is what is taken as fundamental by behaviourist psychologists,[2] who in essence make their research program out of correlating behavioural inputs v_N with behavioural outputs $v_N^{a^*}$ and study some tendencies – "conditioning" – in the evolution of $d(\cdot)$ (see Watson, 1913). We, however, shall be undaunted by the relative inaccessibility of internal mental states, as they are in principle revealable up to the observer's own perception of the world and their skill in eliciting truthful reports by the subjects of their mental state,[3] and formulate a theory of how behaviour is generated by decisions.

Theory of choice, acts, behaviour

To "close" our theory of the psychology of behaviour we must posit a theory of decision, how the individual makes a decision about which course of action $a \in 2^{A'}$ to take on the basis of their understanding $g(H')$ of the objects and events of reality $H' \subset \rho(v_N)$ contained within their perception of a particular environment v_N. If they are to do so then they first will need to be able to isolate the *implications* which are attendant upon the selection of said particular course of action, the outcomes they *think* will follow their course of action.

Definition 10 (Implications of acts). The implications g_a the individual construes of any given act $a \in 2^A$ are the relations $g_a \subset g(H')$ which exist within a *directed* chain of relations, (to abuse notation) $\{h_k h_{k+1}\}_{k=0}^K \subset g(H')$ contained within their understanding of their environment $v_N : \rho(v_N) \supset H'$ which includes a percept $h \in a$ of part of a potential action, that is,

$$g_a = \left\{ R_{hh'} \in g(H') : hh' \in \{h_k h_{k+1}\}_{k=0}^K \subset g(H') \,\&\, h_0 \in a \right\} \quad (3.6)$$

The implications of actions $a \in 2^{A'}$ form chains throughout $g(H')$ which include any of the types of connections proposed by Hume (1777) – resemblance, contiguity, cause and effect – with the proviso that these connections contain a direction equal to the direction of the chains originating with some part of an action $h_0 \in a$. Here we follow the convention that an undirected link contains *both* directions and that those directions are symmetric, that is, $R_{hh'} \in g(H')$ and $R_{h'h} \in g(H')$ and $R_{hh'} = R_{h'h}$. A relation $R_{hh'} \in g(H')$ cannot be included in the implications g_a an individual construes to attend upon a course of action a if it only contains the direction opposite the direction of the chains originating with some part of an action $h_0 \in a$. The chains of implications $g_a \subset g(H')$ thus represent the outcomes the individual *thinks*, *believes* (Shackle, 1969; Taleb, 2007) will attend upon their actions, based on their personal constructs $g(H) \supset g(H')$ (Kelly, 1963), their worldview.

An important generalisation of this concept (which does not greatly affect the structure of the rest of the theory) accounts for the likelihood that the considerations which are relevant for deciding behaviour either consciously or (particularly) subconsciously might terminate as well as originate at elements of a particular course of action. Behaviour might be the "then" in "if-then" connections in the individual's mind as well as

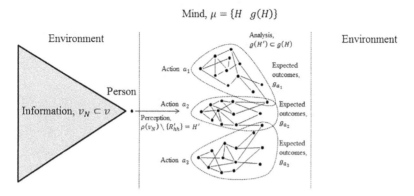

Figure 3.8 Identifying implications of actions a_1, a_2, a_3, the outcomes the individual *thinks* will attend upon them.

the "if", and g_a thus generalised would represent the "predicate conditions" for behaviour to be decided upon as well as the implications, the expected outcomes, of that behaviour. This generalisation is important for understanding rapid-response, impulsive, and emotional behaviour amongst other things.[4]

But not every action $a \subset A$ of which the individual is aware will be actually available to them. Certain actions $a \subset A$ do not satisfy physical and institutional constraints imposed on what acts may be selected and what acts may not. The actions which do satisfy all constraints are said to be feasible acts.

Definition 11 (Feasibility of an action). An action $a \in 2^A$ is said to be feasible, $a \in B$, if it is included within a set $B \subset 2^{A'}$ of potential actions $A' \subset A$ in the particular situation which satisfy certain constraints upon behaviour (that is, B defines a set of subsets of A', a set of feasible actions).

The set of feasible courses of action thus construed is broadly consonant with Amartya Sen's (1999) notion of a "capabilities" set. It is the set of courses of action which the individual is capable of implementing. How now is the individual to be guided by their thinking $g(H')$ about the expected outcomes $g_a \subset g(H')$ to attend on the various courses of action $a \in 2^{A'}$ available to them to choose between the various courses of action $B \subset 2^{A'}$ which are feasible?

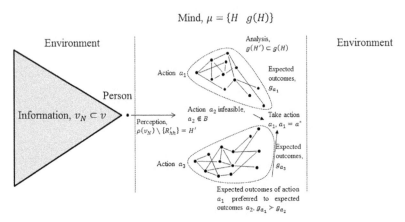

Mind, $\mu = \{H \quad g(H)\}$

Figure 3.9 Decision making, choosing the action a_1 which is associated with the most preferable implications out of all feasible actions.

Let us consider the function of the language in which $g(H)$ is expressed. Our language describes our world and our relation to it, and it must therefore express our normative reaction to it, our range of feelings about the world positive, negative and ambivalent. If language did not contain symbols expressing these feelings, it would not help us describe our relation to the world.

We may hypothesise then that the language in which $g(H)$ is expressed implies a "preference structure" on itself, representing the notion that certain sets of relations are more preferable than others.

Definition 12 (Preferences). Preference $\succeq$ is a pre-ordering defined on subsets $g' \in 2^{g(H)}$ of personal knowledge which is implied by the semantics of the syntax, the language, in which those subsets $g' \in 2^{g(H)}$ of knowledge $g(H)$ are constructed. That is, $g(H) \Rightarrow \succeq \circ 2^{g(H)}$. If both $g' \succeq g''$ and $g'' \succeq g'$ are true then $g' \sim g''$, and if $g' \succeq g''$ but *not* $g'' \succeq g'$ then $g' \succ g''$. The ordering $g' \succeq g''$ is to be read *the thoughts contained within g' are more preferable than those contained within g''* (*strictly* preferable if $g' \succ g''$).

To put it in the manner a philosopher would, though more generally than the strict art-theory definition given it in modern times, the preference structure $\succeq \circ 2^{g(H)}$ reflects, and emerges from, the *aesthetical* content of the relations $R_{hh'} \in g(H)$. The aesthetics of subsets $g' \subset g(H)$ of construed relations between objects of reality within our understanding of the world $g(H)$ are something given by the conscious experience of the world and how it feels (Burke, 1757). These aesthetics are reflected in the normative structure of the language in which our mental networks are expressed.

The preference structure $\succeq \circ 2^{g(H)}$ implied by our aesthetics need not be well defined for every pair of subsets g', $g'' \subset g(H)^5$ as it may be difficult to form a definite binary comparison of the relative aesthetical content of the sets of relations g' and g''. We will return to this below (theorem 3) for instead of being a dead-end, this possible ill-definedness is one source for a theory of indecision.

We now have a definition of the actions available to the individual (9), a definition of how the individual thinks about those acts (10), a definition of which alternatives are actually feasible (11), and a criterion for making judgments between sets of relations within $g(H)$ (12), of which the implications g_a of any action are one kind. We are thus in a position to set down a theory of choice among actions, and thus behaviour.

Theorem 2 (The Theory of Choice). *If in a particular environment v_N, individuals select that feasible action $a^* \in 2^A$ which is associated with the set of implications g_a able to be ranked against any of the implications associated with any other feasible actions and which is not weakly less preferable than the implications associated with any other feasible actions (the Socratic axiom), then individuals select that course of action which is feasible, and associated with the most preferable set of implications out of all feasible actions. That is, a^* satisfies the following equation:*

$$a^* = \{a \in B : g_a \succ g_{a'} \, \forall a' \in B\} \tag{3.7}$$

where $g_a \subset g(H')$, $H' = \rho\,(v_N)\backslash\{R_{hh'}\}$, and $a' \neq a$.

The Socratic axiom is that no individual acts contrary to their knowledge of their best interests, which is posited by Socrates in both Plato's *Republic*

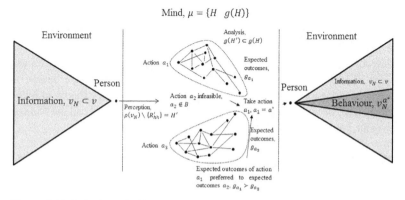

Figure 3.10 Behaviour decided upon by the individual and realised in the world.

and Xenophon's *Memorabilia*. Acting against one's interests is a problem of incomplete knowledge. The elicited knowledge $g(H') \subset g(H)$ which would support acting according to "virtue" must be elicited at any particular point in time. Hence knowledge *is* virtue. It is not particularly productive to debate this supposition, for we interpret here the axiom quite weakly as supposing that no individual acts contrary to their best interest given *their* personal knowledge of how and why to act in the world, *their* personal morality, *their* set of rules for behaviour and *their* state of mind at any particular point in time. It is productive to suppose the Socratic axiom, for it gives us theorem 2 and equation 3.7.

Thus we complete our basic theory of the psychological process and behaviour. Note how our theory of behaviour encompasses the whole of this process, our decisions are based on our assessment (formed consciously or subconsciously) of our perception of our environment. At a neural level, memories encoded in our hippocampus and emotions and visceral urges originating in our amygdala are combining with sensory input from all parts of the brain to be referred to the ethics encoded in our prefrontal cortex for regulation and decision (Sapolsky, 2017). Behaviour arises from our application of our personal knowledge of the world expressed in our mental networks to our perception of the information in our environment. It is a reflection of our application of personal constructs to reality (Kelly, 1963), and thus a reflection of our personality, offering us a means to infer personality from behaviour if we have a specific typology and theory of its interaction with behaviour in mind in the style of Jung (1921), Briggs, Myers and Myers (1980) or Riso and Hudson (1996).

Theory of indecision and decision paralysis

Theorem 2 gives us a theory of decision, behaviour, and why choices are made. But we can also, using this theorem, in particular the well-definedness or not of equation 3.7, derive a theory of why choices are *not* made. Our view of the psychological process and of how behaviour is determined gives us both a theory of choice and a theory of non-choice, a theory of action, and a theory of non-action, a theory of decision, and a theory of indecision. The theory of *indecision* is developed in what we shall call the "'make up your mind/checkmate' theorem".

Theorem 3 (The "make up your mind/checkmate" theorem). *Choices made according to equation 3.7 are well defined, that is,*

$$\exists a : a = \{a \in B : g_a \succ g_{a'} \, \forall a' \in B\} \tag{3.8}$$

if and only if preferences $\succeq \circ 2^{g(H)}$ *can be established over the understanding of the particular environment* $g(H')$ *(where* $\rho\ (v_N) \setminus \{R_{hh'}\} = H'$*) such that:*

1 The set $B \subset 2^{A'}$ of feasible actions within the set of subsets of potential behaviour A' in a particular situation v_N is non-empty. That is, $B \neq \emptyset$.

2 There is an act $a \in B$ the implications of which the preferability of the implications of no other feasible act $a' \in B$ cannot be established with respect to. That is, $\nexists a' \in B : \geqslant \circ 2^{g(H)} \nRightarrow g_a \gtrless g_{a'} \lor g_{a'} \gtrless g_a \lor g_a \sim g_{a'}$.

3 There is such a feasible act $a \in B$ which the implications of no other feasible act $a' \in B$ can be established as weakly preferred to (i.e. preferred or indifferent) its implications. That is, $\nexists a' \in B : \geqslant \circ 2^{g(H)} \Rightarrow g_{a'} \gtrless g_a$.

The interesting thing about this theorem is not so much what it requires as what it does *not* require. It does not require (condition 2) that the preferences $\succeq \circ 2^{g(H)}$ be complete in the sense that every alternative is able to be ranked against every other. It only requires the one act to be able to be ranked against all the others. And it does not require (condition 3) that there be internal relations of a particular type among all alternatives, only that one alternative in particular can be established to be not less preferable against the others. Intransitive cycles ($g_{a^1} \succeq g_{a^2}$, $g_{a^2} \succeq g_{a^3}$ but $g_{a^3} \succeq g_{a^1}$) may exist, but they will only lead to undefined choices if there is no "tiebreaker" which can be established strictly preferable to all implications in the cycle (i.e. there is no $g_a \succ g_{a^1}$, g_{a^2} & g_{a^3}). It may in fact be the case that preference $\succeq \circ 2^{g(H)}$ suffices only to determine that one action's implications are preferable to all others $g_a \succ g_{a'} \forall a' \in B$, and nothing else, and yet it is sufficient for choices to be well defined. This fact means comparatively little knowledge and information is required for an individual to be able to act in the world.

Further, the conditions of this theorem tell us exactly why no choice is made if that is the case. It may be that, as the old saying goes, we are comparing "apples and oranges" and cannot establish the preferability between an act we would otherwise take, and some other action (breaking condition 2) because we cannot establish the relation between some ideas. That is, we may have two acts g_a and $g_{a'}$ for which we can establish neither that $g_a \succeq g_{a'}$ nor $g_{a'} \succeq g_a$, and we may not actually know our preferences. The classic case of non-comparability of course is that of Hamlet, trying to establish whether the implications of killing the king (possible regicide against God's anointed King, therefore eternal damnation), are preferable or less preferable to the implications of not killing the king (possible failure to take action against an adulterous, incestuous regicide, therefore eternal damnation).

Alternatively, it may be the case that we cannot establish a strict preference between two alternatives, which would therefore be indifferent to one another $g_a \sim g_{a'}$, and there is no "tiebreaker" to establish a strictly more preferred alternative (breaking condition 2).[6] Tacitus relates in the *Histories* that Vespasian during the year of the four emperors was paralysed by indifference when considering the outcomes of choosing to continue the Jewish War in Syria or returning to challenge Vitellius for the tribunician authority in Italy, and it took Mucianus' entreaties to change his considerations enough that he could eventually decide for the latter. Like Buridan's ass we may be paralysed by our indifference between two haystacks and require more information to make a decision.[7]

But further, this theory of choice demonstrates that above all, a choice must be available to an individual if they are to behave (condition 1). It may be an academic problem whether this is ever in fact not true, for we may define it to be the case always that $\emptyset \in A'$, and define "no choice" by this "choice" *a la* the "status quo"/"outside option" of game theoretical models. Nevertheless the point still stands that an individual may choose to not to act at all, or the choice function may be not well defined unless we include non-action as a potential action $\emptyset \in A'$. So a property of theorem 3 is that we can explain an individual not making a decision not only as an issue of "making up one's mind" – an "indecision" theorem – but also as an issue of not having any feasible option available.

3.4   Mental evolution and the dynamics of the mind

The theory of the mind, psychology and behaviour we have proposed thus far may be, if one accepts its predicates, a little unsettling. It implies that we are not the masters of our own thoughts. We cannot greatly control them, they emerge from the interaction of our mental networks and the world mediated by perception. We are, therefore, by extension, not greatly the masters of our own behaviour, being as it is a reflection of our personality.

However, we can, if we accept the phenomenological "I" has such influence, change the basis of our thought, change the *way* we think about the world. The mind, our mental networks $\mu = \{H \quad g(H)\}$ which is the basis of our thought and behaviour evolves over time by the incorporation of new connections into our understanding of the relations $g(H)$ of the objects and events in the world H and the decay of existing ones. The dynamics of the mind, of mental networks μ, are a point at which indeterminacy potentially enters into our theory, an indeterminacy which cannot but be reconciled by the phenomenological "I" as discussed previously (p. 9). The first indeterminacy arises in the sources of new connections, and the second in the process whereby each is incorporated into the mind.

The sources of new connections are, potentially, two, and were in fact the cause of one of the more famous disagreements between Kant and Hume. Hume in his earlier writings held that the only sources of new connections in the mind was "sense data", the perception thereof. Kant disagreed and instead could be understood to be suggesting that we may also *create* connections between objects and events without their having been presented in sense-data. We might make "*a priori* synthetic statements", which we here would attribute to the phenomenological "I". There are thus two sources of new connections to be incorporated into mental networks:

1   Genuinely creative thought: A bisociation, a thought $R_{hh'}$, exists for no reason other than the "I" thinking it, in contradiction to the principle of sufficient reason (Koestler, 1964; Bergson, 1946; Shackle, 1972).
2   Suggestion by perception of apparent relations: A relation $R_{hh'}$ is contained within the set $\{R_{hh'}\} \subset \rho\,(v_N)$ of apparent relations between the objects and events in the environment v_N.

If one does not believe the phenomenological "I" has any input into the psychological process, and that that process is entirely determined, then one simply eliminates 1. as a source of mental evolution.

It is interesting here to note a reflexivity of sorts between action a^* and mental networks μ. If action manifests in behaviour $v_N^{a^*}$ which is part of the "sense-data" of the environment, part of the information v_N and if it interacts with that information, it is possible that the individual's actions a^* might cause there to be information $v' \subset v_N$ in their environment v_N which would suggest apparent relations $R_{hh'} \in \rho\,(v_N)$ between the objects and events in the environment. That is, it may be the case that

$$a^* \Rightarrow \exists v' \subset v_N : \rho\,(v' \subset v_N) \supset R_{hh'} \tag{3.9}$$

The most obvious examples of such behaviour are to be found in developmental psychology, and the actions by which we learn. Jean Piaget (1923) observed that children developed their "schema" of the world, their understanding of their place in and relation to it and the language to describe it (their "personal knowledge" $g(H)$) by simply asking "why" and awaiting a response by which an adult would suggest a reason for the objects and events in their environment. As we mature we increasingly substitute this for the reading of books, conversations and classes. And as we mature yet further we substitute it for reasoning and calculation (Newell et al., 1958, 1962; Simon, 1969, 1998) and more developed forms of experimentation (Dewey, 1910). But the principle remains the same; we are motivated to act a^* to search for information $v' \subset v_N$ in our environment or to create it which will present apparent relations $R_{hh'}$ between objects and events in our environment to our perception which, if incorporated into our mental networks cause our personal knowledge to grow, and us thereby to learn. It is this process that, replicated in the workings and calculations of a machine we call "machine learning" (Samuel, 1959).

So thus we have the sources of new connections which might cause mental networks to evolve and grow. But having these presented to the mind is not sufficient for mental evolution, they must be incorporated, $R_{hh'} \in g(H)$, into those networks for personal knowledge to grow. As Newman (1870) might have said, personal knowledge grows by "assent" to new connections. This is the second potential source of indeterminacy in our theory, for the assent to new connections is the province of the phenomenological "I". This creates a *likelihood* that new connections presented to the mind will be incorporated into mental networks.

Definition 13 (The likelihood of incorporating $R_{hh'}$). The likelihood $p(R_{hh'} \in g(H))$ of a particular relation $R_{hh'}$ between objects and events being incorporated into the individual's understanding of the world $g(H)$ is given by an individual-specific mapping $p : R \rightarrow [0, 1]$ from the space of relations R to the likelihood of incorporation, where a likelihood of one, $p(R_{hh'} \in g(H)) = 1$, represents certainty of incorporation and a likelihood of zero, $p(R_{hh'} \in g(H)) = 0$, represents certainty of non-incorporation. If the relation is already part of $g(H)$ it is certain it will be included within $g(H)$, that is, $R_{hh} \in g(H) \Rightarrow p(R_{hh} \in g(H)) = 1$.

This likelihood is not to be interpreted as a traditional probability, for we cannot in good faith interpret it in a strict frequentist sense. It is more akin to likelihood in the common sensibility, the inverse of "surprise" if you will (see Shackle, 1969 and Taleb, 2007).

So as new connections are presented to the individual and assented to, incorporated into the mind, $R_{hh'} \in g(H)$, the mind evolves. Mental networks grow at the margin extending personal knowledge (Polanyi, 1958), extending upon an existing base of knowledge (Calvin, 1997, p.33) to inform our thinking about the relations of the objects and events of the world, and to therefore inform our decisions about how to act. As David Hume put it in his later work, ceding somewhat to Kant:

Nothing is more free than the imagination of man; and though it cannot exceed that original stock of ideas, furnished by the internal and

The psychology of behaviour 33

external senses, it has unlimited power of mixing, compounding, separating, and dividing these ideas, in all the varieties of fiction and vision.

(Hume, 1777, p.31)

This evolution underlies the development of science, technology, art and literature (Koestler, 1964), and the growth of personal knowledge has facilitated the entire history of social and economic development (Hayek, 1988).

Though an ultimately indeterminate process which can only be resolved by the phenomenological "I", we can draw on a number of theories to elaborate certain factors which influence the likelihood the individual will incorporate a particular relation $R_{hh'}$ generated by creative thought or apparent in the perception of sense-data.

First we can say that out of the space of all possible links to be made R, any particular link $R_{hh'}$ is more likely to be made if it is suggested by the perception of sense-data to the individual, that is, if it is an apparent relation between the objects of reality h, $h' \in H'$. The reason for this is straightforward: if it is more definite we are even aware of a new relation it must be more definite we shall assent to it.

Definition 14 (The law of suggestion). The likelihood $p(R_{hh'} \in g(H))$ of a relation $R_{hh'}$ being incorporated within the individual's understanding of the objects of reality $g(H)$ is increasing with respect to the perception, $R_{hh'} \in H' \subset \rho(v_N)$ or not $R_{hh'} \notin \rho(v_N)$ of that relation in the individual's environment, that is

$$\frac{\partial p(R_{hh'} \in g(H))}{\partial I(R_{hh'} \in \rho(v_N))} \geq 0 \qquad (3.10)$$

where

$$I(R_{hh'} \in \rho(v_N)) = \begin{cases} 1 & \text{if } R_{hh'} \in \rho(v_N) \\ 0 & \text{if } R_{hh'} \notin \rho(v_N) \end{cases} \qquad (3.11)$$

It has also been hypothesised, and is intuitive, that we are resistant to change the "core" of who we are, the "core" concepts on which our understanding of the world is based. George Kelly (1963) suggests in the organisation corollary of his personal construct psychology that certain constructs are more important than others, more central to our understanding of the world. To change these is to alter to a relatively greater extent our knowledge of the world and the degree to which it "makes sense" (is logically consistent). Because this is uncomfortable,[8] it is less likely a new relation $R_{hh'}$ will be incorporated into $g(H)$ the more "core" that relation will be within the system of personal constructs $g(H)$.[9]

Definition 15 (The law of resistance at the core). The likelihood $p(R_{hh'} \in g(H))$ of a relation $R_{hh'}$ being incorporated within the individual's understanding of the world $g(H)$ is decreasing in the network centralities $C_{g(H)}(h)$ and $C_{g(H)}(h')$ of the objects or events it would connect, $h, h' \in H$ (where $C_{g(H)}(\cdot)$ is some metric of network centrality[10] in $g(H)$) that is

$$\frac{\partial p(R_{hh'} \in g(H))}{\partial c\left(C_{g(H)}(h) \quad C_{g(H)}(h')\right)} \leq 0 \tag{3.12}$$

where $c(\cdot)$ is some monotonically increasing function of the network centralities $C_{g(H)}(h)$ and $C_{g(H)}(h')$.

A second source of discomfort born of considering new links $R_{hh'}$ for incorporation into $g(H)$, proposed by Leon Festinger (1957), is cognitive dissonance. Cognitive dissonance exists wherever in one's analysis of a particular environment $g(H')$ there are relations (say, $R_{hh'}$ and $R_{h''h'''}$) which contradict each other and are likely to cause discomfort. If individuals, as Festinger (1957) argues, seek to avoid dissonance because it is uncomfortable, they are more likely to reject new relations $R_{hh'}$ between the objects of reality the more they are dissonant with their understanding of a particular situation.[11]

Definition 16 (The law of resistance to dissonance). The likelihood $p(R_{hh'} \in g(H))$ of a relation $R_{hh'}$ being incorporated within the individual's understanding of the objects of reality $g(H)$ is decreasing in the degree $|\{R_{h''h'''} \in g(H') : R_{hh'} \Rightarrow \neg R_{h''h'''}\}|$ to which that relation is dissonant with (approximately implies the opposite of) other relations within the individual's understanding $g(H')$ of their particular environment H', that is

$$\frac{\partial p(R_{hh'} \in g(H))}{\partial |\{R_{h''h'''} \in g(H') : R_{hh'} \Rightarrow \neg R_{h''h'''}\}|} \leq 0 \tag{3.13}$$

Immediately we can demonstrate the equivalence of this law to Festinger's (1957) second proposal, that individuals seek consonance.

Corollary 2 (The law of attraction to consonance). *The likelihood $p(R_{hh'} \in g(H))$ of a relation $R_{hh'}$ being incorporated within the individual's understanding of the objects of reality $g(H)$ is non-decreasing in the degree*

$|\{R_{h''h'''} \in g(H') : R_{hh'} \Rightarrow \neg R_{h''h'''}\}|$ *to which that relation is consonant with (does not imply the opposite of) other relations within the individual's understanding $g(H')$ of their particular environment H', that is*

$$\frac{\partial p(R_{hh'} \in g(H))}{\partial |\{R_{h''h'''} \in g(H') : R_{hh'} \not\Rightarrow \neg R_{h''h'''}\}|} \geq 0 \qquad (3.14)$$

So, in summary, the likelihood that any new connection $R_{hh'}$ will be incorporated into an individual's understanding of reality $g(H)$ is increasing in its having been suggested to the individual, decreasing in the centrality of that connection to the understanding $g(H)$ and decreasing in the degree of dissonance of that connection with understanding of a particular environment $g(H')$.[12] This establishes the factors at play in a sort of psychological "wave function". The possibility of genuinely creative thought however distinguishes "the" psychological wave function as we might not even be able to conceive of the state space before it exists (Shackle, 1969, 1972; Taleb, 2007). But what of the decay of existing connections within $g(H)$?

It is an immediate corollary of the second law of thermodynamics that entropy (disorder) increases in all physical systems in the absence of the degradation of free energy (Georgescu-Roegen, 1971; Schneider and Kay, 1994; Raine et al., 2006) that the neural correlates of $R_{hh} \in g(H)$ will decay over time, unless energy is expended in their maintenance. We know that neural networks decay when they aren't used and get stronger the more they are used (Sapolsky, 2017; Kandel et al., 2013). At a mental level, this would manifest in a metric $s(\cdot)$ reflecting the "strength" of a connection $R_{hh'} \in g(H)$ tending to decay toward zero, meaning it no longer exists in understanding $g(H)$, it is "forgotten".

Definition 17 (The law of entropy, or memory decay). The strength of any connection $R_{hh'} \in g(H)$ within an individual's understanding $g(H)$ of the objects and events in the world H is an individual specific mapping $s : g(H) \to \mathbb{R}_+$ from their understanding $g(H)$ to the positive real numbers $\mathbb{R}_+$ such that a strength of zero means that connection no longer exists in their mind $s(R_{hh'}) = 0 \Rightarrow R_{hh'} \notin g(H')$. This strength decays over time $t \in \mathbb{R}$

$$\frac{\partial s(R_{hh'})}{\partial t} \leq 0 \,\forall\, t \in \mathbb{R} \qquad (3.15)$$

at a rate which is slowed by (decreasing in) the number of times $T(R_{hh'} \in g(H')) \in \mathbb{Z}$ that relation is made in the process of thought

$g(H')$, (the number of times it is "refreshed")

$$\frac{\partial}{\partial T\left(R_{hh'} \in g\left(H'\right)\right)} \frac{\partial s\left(R_{hh'}\right)}{\partial t} = \frac{\partial^2 s\left(R_{hh'}\right)}{\partial T\left(R_{hh'} \in g\left(H'\right)\right)\partial t}$$

$$\leq 0\,\forall\, T\left(R_{hh'} \in g\left(H'\right)\right) \in \mathbb{Z} \tag{3.16}$$

and is increasing only in the number of times $T\left(R_{hh'} \in g\left(H'\right)\right) \in \mathbb{Z}$ that relation is made in analysis, the process of thought (i.e. through the expenditure of energy)

$$\partial s\left(R_{hh'}\right) \geq 0 \Leftrightarrow \partial T\left(R_{hh'} \in g\left(H'\right)\right) \geq 0 \tag{3.17}$$

The notion of "strength" $s(\cdot)$ will be left undefined here but for the common sensibility of the notion of "strength" in memory. The "strength" of memory is the inverse of its "vagueness". As the strength of memory decays through time, the memory $R_{hh'} \in g(H)$ tends toward a state where it shall no longer be included among all other memories an individual has.

There is a connection between these laws governing the dynamics of the mind and the "neural Darwinism" hypothesis. Edelman (1987) suggests that selective pressures are exerted upon neural substructures adapted epigenetically. Epigenetic adaptation at the neural level manifests here at the mental level as new connections $R_{hh'}$ are incorporated into $g(H)$, $R_{hh'} \in g(H)$, and our laws of incorporation elaborate the likelihood they will be so incorporated. The entropic decay of these relations if they are not consistently elicited manifests at the mental level in the deselection of their neural correlates by the neural evolutionary process. The brain, vicariously the mind, thus becomes an arena for evolutionary pressures, growing at the margin to incorporate new ideas, new connections, and decaying where those structures are not of use to the individual in understanding the world.

Notes

1. In Descartes' (1637 and 1641) dualist system by contrast, this is the *only* object acts consist of.
2. Strictly speaking, it is more accurate to say they take the mapping $d_v : V_N \to 2^{V_a}$, mentioned in the proof of theorem 1 to be fundamental, for they base their studies on observed behaviour rather than individuals' choices *per se*.
3. The neuropsychologist, correlating brain function with mental states rather than observed behaviour, faces a similar constraint.
4. Formally, we would have $g_a = \{R_{hh'} \in g(H'):hh' \in \{h_k h_{k+1}\}_{(k=0)}^{K} \subset g(H')\ \&\ h_0 \lor h_K \in a\}$. Neurophysiologically we know this to be reflected in the structure of the brain. We know that emotion precedes action for signals from the nervous system that pass through the amygdala (the "emotional centre") before passing

The psychology of behaviour 37

even to the sensory cortex. But we also know the prefrontal cortex is often activated to simulate the future course of events.

5. To put it formally, $\succeq \circ 2^{g(H)}$ might not be complete: it might not be the case that $g' \succeq g'' \vee g'' \succeq g' \vee g' \sim g'' \; \forall \; g', g'' \in 2^{g(H)}$.

6. Both Earl (1986b) and Leibenstein (1976) draw attention to this possibility, the former arguing the need therefore established for a "constitution" of hierarchical rules for deciding disputes by "tiebreakers", the latter arguing for the existence of a "selective" rationality to serve the same purpose when rules cannot establish sufficient preferabilities to allow for decision.

7. Sonja Amadae (2016) notes how this would cause a failure of the conditions required to solve the Church-Turing stopping problem in an Artificial Intelligence.

8. M. Scott Peck, building on George Kelly's pathological psychology attributing neurosis to lack of ability to make sense of the world as mental maps change, famously spoke of the "healthiness of depression", depression being the discomfort experienced as our maps $g(H)$ evolve to make sense of new situations and new sense-data. The common theme to the stories told by the psychoanalyst Stephen Grosz (2013), is of people suffering because they cannot make sense of, understand, their environment V_N and what is happening to them v_N.

9. Peter Earl (1986a,b) has made use of George Kelly's analogy of people "as scientists" trying to understand their world to draw parallels to the scientific philosophy of Imre Lakatos. Lakatos (1968–1969) argues that within any body of scientific work there are certain theories which are more important, prior to others, central to the body of work, more "axiomatic" and less testable, and that individuals working within that scientific discipline will be more resistant to change these for the implications it would have for understanding.

10. For instance, degree centrality, betweenness centrality, or the more sophisticated eigenvector centrality (which, however, requires $g(H)$ to be a matrix in metric space).

11. Akerlof and Dickens (1982) provide a characteristically neoclassical economic perspective on cognitive dissonance in which the individual optimises their "utility" in their selection, *inter alia* of "beliefs" – the probability distribution they construe over states of the world – thus "optimally" trading cognitive dissonance off against cognitive consonance.

12. We might hypothesise, taking the distribution $p(\cdot)$ over R a means by which it can be transformed into a distribution $p^g : R \to [0, 1]$ of likelihoods $p^g(g(H))$ of future configurations $g(H)$ of the individual's understanding. This would be the wave function over future states of mind $g(H)$ in the same manner the physical wave function represents likelihoods over future states of physical systems (Feynman, 1965; Kent, 2012). This wave function over future states of mind (vicariously, decision) is what is treated of by quantum models of cognition (Busemeyer et al., 2006; Busemeyer and Buruza, 2012). What the formalism here does with our theories of $p(\cdot)$ and $p^g(\cdot)$ is to elaborate the psychological factors underlying their form where quantum models will tend to focus on specifying their transition through time using quantum state transition mathematics.

References

Akerlof, G., Dickens, W., 1982. The economic consequences of cognitive dissonance. *American Economic Review* 72 (3), 307–319.

38   The psychology of behaviour

Amadae, S., 2016. Computability of rational action. In: Seibt, J., Nørskov, M., Andersen, S. (Eds.), *What Social Robots Can and Should Do. Vol. 290 of Frontiers in Artificial Intelligence and Applications*. IOS Press, Amsterdam, pp. 257–267.

Bergson, H., 1946. *The Creative Mind*. Citadel Press, New York.

Boulding, K., 1961. *The Image*. University of Michigan Press, Ann Arbor.

Briggs Myers, I., Myers, P., 1980. *Gifts Differing*. Nicholas Brealey Publishing, London.

Burke, E., 1757. *A Philosophical Enquiry into the Sublime and Beautiful*, 2nd Edition. Oxford's World Classics. Oxford University Press, Oxford.

Busemeyer, J., Buruza, P., 2012. *Quantum Models of Cognition and Decision*. Cambridge University Press, Cambridge.

Busemeyer, J., Wang, Z., Townsend, J., 2006. Quantum dynamics of human decision-making. *Journal of Mathematical Psychology* 50, 220–241.

Calvin, W., 1997. *How Brains Think*. Phoenix, London.

Descartes, R., 1637 & 1641. *Discourse on Method and the Meditations*. Penguin, London.

Dewey, J., 1910. *How We Think*. D.C. Heath and Co., Lexington.

Earl, P., 1986a. A behavioural analysis of demand elasticities. *Journal of Economic Studies* 13 (3), 20–37.

Earl, P., 1986b. *Lifestyle Economics*. Harvester Wheatsheaf, Brighton.

Edelman, G., 1987. *Neural Darwinism*. Basic Books, New York.

Festinger, L., 1957. *A Theory of Cognitive Dissonance*. Stanford University Press, Stanford.

Feynman, R., 1965. *The Character of Physical Law*. Penguin, London.

Georgescu-Roegen, N., 1971. *The Entropy Law and the Economic Process*. Harvard University Press, Cambridge, MA.

Grosz, S., 2013. *The Examined Life*. Vintage, London.

Hayek, F., 1952. *The Sensory Order*. University of Chicago Press, Chicago.

Hayek, F., 1988. *The Fatal Conceit*. Vol. 1 of *The Collected Works of F.A. Hayek*. University of Chicago Press, Chicago.

Hume, D., 1777. *An Enquiry Concerning Human Understanding*, 2nd Edition. Hackett Publishing Company, Cambridge.

Jung, C., 1921. *Psychological Types*. Routledge, London.

Kandel, E., Schwartz, J., Jessell, T., Siegelbaum, S., Hudspeth, A. (Eds.), 2013. *Principles of Neural Science*, 5th Edition. McGraw-Hill, New York.

Kelly, G., 1963. *A Theory of Personality*. Norton, New York.

Kent, A., 2012. Real world interpretations of quantum theory. *Foundations of Physics* 42, 421–435.

Koestler, A., 1964. *The Act of Creation*. Pan Books Ltd, London.

Lakatos, I., 1968–1969. Criticism and the methodology of scientific research programmes. *Proceedings of the Aristotelian Society* 69 (New Series, 1968–1969), 149–186.

Leibenstein, H., 1976. *Beyond Economic Man*. Harvard University Press, Cambridge, MA.

Mastrogiorgio, A., Petracca, E., 2016. *Model-Based Reasoning in Science and Technology*. Springer, New York City, Ch. Embodying rationality, pp. 219–237.

Merleau-Ponty, M., 1945. *Phenomenology of Perception*. Routledge, London.

Merleau-Ponty, M., 1948. *The World of Perception*. Routledge, London.

Newell, A., Shaw, J., Simon, H., 1958. Elements of a theory of human problem solving. *Psychological Review* 65 (3), 151–166.

Newell, A., Shaw, J., Simon, H., 1962. *Contemporary Approaches to Creative Thinking*. Behavioral Science Series. Atherton Press, New York, Ch. The processes of creative thinking, pp. 63–119.

Newman, J., 1870. *An Essay in Aid of a Grammar of Assent*. Oxford University Press, Oxford.

Piaget, J., 1923. *The Language and Thought of the Child*. Routledge, London.

Polanyi, M., 1958. *Personal Knowledge*. Routledge and Kegan Paul, London.

Popper, K., 1934. *Logic of Scientific Discovery*. Routledge, London.

Raine, A., Foster, J., Potts, J., 2006. The new entropy law and the economic process. *Ecological Complexity* 3, 354–360.

Riso, D., Hudson, R., 1996. *Personality Types*. Houghton Mifflin, Boston.

Samuel, A., 1959. Some studies in machine learning using the game of checkers. *IBM Journal of Research and Development* 3 (3), 210–229.

Sapolsky, R., 2017. *Behave*. Penguin, London.

Schneider, E., Kay, J., 1994. Life as a manifestation of the second law of thermodynamics. *Mathematical and Computer Modelling* 19 (6–8), 25–48.

Sen, A., 1993. Positional objectivity. *Philosophy and Public Affairs* 22 (2), 126–145.

Sen, A., 1999. *Commodities and Capabilities*. Oxford University Press, Oxford.

Shackle, G., 1969. *Decision Order and Time*, 2nd Edition. Cambridge University Press, Cambridge.

Shackle, G., 1972. *Epistemics and Economics*. Transaction Publishers, Piscataway.

Shannon, C., 1948a. A mathematical theory of communication. *Bell System Technical Journal* 27 (3), 379–423.

Shannon, C., 1948b. A mathematical theory of communication. *Bell System Technical Journal* 27 (4), 623–666.

Simon, H., 1956. Rational choice and the structure of the environment. *Psychological Review* 63 (2), 129–138.

Simon, H., 1969. *The Sciences of the Artificial*. MIT Press, Cambridge, MA.

Simon, H., 1998. Discovering explanations. *Minds and Machines* 8, 7–37.

Taleb, N., 2007. *The Black Swan*. Penguin, London.

Watson, J., 1913. Psychology as the behaviorist views it. *Psychological Review* 20, 158–177.

Wittgenstein, L., 1921. *Tractatus Logico-Philosophicus*. Routledge, London.

Wittgenstein, L., 1953. *Philosophical Investigations*, 4th Edition. Wiley-Blackwell, Chicester.

4 Reasons, rules, society and motivation in the psychological process

On the face of it, the theory of choice, theorem 2 may appear to be the same theory of behaviour as that of neoclassical economics, that theory (Debreu, 1959; Mas-Collel et al., 1995; Rubinstein, 2006; Jehle and Reny, 2011) too being one of constrained optimisation of preference. However, this resemblance is only on the face of things. There is a truth to that theory, but the theory we have proposed places that truth within a vision of the psychological process as a whole and so integrates a variety of psychological and behavioural phenomena. The remainder of this work is concerned with elaborating how the theory does this. The present chapter begins this task by showing how behaviour theorised by theorem 2 may arise from thinking in the traditional "linguistic" sense, from cognitive rule-following, from their coexistence, how social factors affect these processes, and how preferences emerge.

4.1 Mental networks as expressing reason

The first, and most intuitive interpretation of mental networks $\mu = \{H \; g(H)\}$ is that they express chains of thought expressed in linguistic symbols. That is to say, they express the syntax of the sentences spoken within the "inner conversation" (Archer, 2003) if you will, the conversation we reveal to others by "thinking out loud", and which we struggle to verbalise if it proceeds in symbols (Jung, 1964), or outside conventional language in the "tacit dimension" (Polanyi, 1967). We might conceptualise the basic unit of thought thus as a "sentence equivalent", drawing on the notion of Wittgenstein (Wittgenstein, 1914–1916, 1921; Wittgenstein et al., 1930–1932; Wittgenstein, 1953) that all languages consist of the expression of meaning using "pictures" as symbols.

Definition 18 (Sentence equivalents). A sentence equivalent is a string of symbols $p_1, p_2, \ldots, p_n$ the content of which taken together is semantically equivalent to a sentence $l \in L$ contained within a *potential* (not necessarily extant) linguistic system L.

We can now prove that as long as the linguistic system conforms to certain conditions (which aren't very strenuous), thoughts as expressed in sentence equivalents can be expressed in chains within $g(H)$.

Theorem 4 (Mental networks may express sentence equivalents). *If any linguistic sentence $l \in L$ contained within any potential linguistic system L must express a sequential series of relations between two subjects/ objects then the sentence equivalent p_1, p_2, . . ., p_n of that sentence l may be represented by a chain $\{h_k h_{k+1}\}_{k=0}^{K} \subset g(H)$.*

It takes no particular effort to demonstrate then that "rational" thought can be expressed within mental networks, if they are expressed as linguistic sentences.

Corollary 3 ($g(H')$ may express rational thought). *If any linguistic sentence $l \in L$ expressing rational thought contained within any potential linguistic system L must express a series of relations between two subjects/objects then the sentence equivalent p_1, p_2, . . ., p_n of that rational thought l may be represented by a chain $\{h_k h_{k+1}\}_{k=0}^{K} \subset g(H)$.*

It is difficult to imagine rational thoughts would not meet the conditions of corollary 3. *Ratio decidendi* as they are called in jurisprudence, are sentences which express the *reasons* we would give in constructing a particular *chain* of reasoning, "because/therefore" sentences which express thoughts about cause-and-effect relations $R_{hh'} \supset h \Rightarrow h'$ terminating with some axiomatic statement.[1] So mental networks can express *reason*, when they are applied to analyse a particular environment, $g(H') \subset g(H)$, they support the process of reasoning about the environment $v_N : \rho (v_N) \supset H'$, and behaviour thus emerges from a process of reasoning.

Even when expressing *ratio decidendi* in the form of sentence equivalents, thoughts need not necessarily conform however with normative criterion for "rationality". This is simply a matter of assumption.

If thoughts were to express *ratio decidendi* conforming, for instance, to the criteria of the early Wittgenstein, then their logical form expressed in the sentence equivalents l would have to conform with the logical form of objects and events, and the connections construed thus would have to be verifiable by direct experience (Wittgenstein, 1921; Ayer, 1936; Popper, 1934; Pears, 1971). But we know that many motivating *ratio decidendi* are both critically important and inexpressible in spoken linguistic systems (Polanyi, 1967) or symbolic without conforming to any logical forms in the environment (Jung, 1964). In fact, as we will return to below, it may be necessary for them to be so.

4.2   Mental networks as expressing rules, routines and habit

An alternative, and important interpretation of mental networks $\mu = \{H \quad g(H)\}$ is found in cognitive psychology, where thoughts are conceived of as the operation of different algorithmic rules, and behaviour arises from those rules. Herbert Simon was a pioneer in this area, developing the idea (Simon, 1969)[2] perhaps first proposed by Alan Turing (1950) and von Neumann (1958) that the mind operates in a manner akin to a computer[3] – executing a series of tasks upon the receipt of certain inputs – and that seemingly complex and individuated behaviour can be understood to be the outcome of fairly simple rules operating on the information contained within the environment (Simon, 1956).[4] Indeed, Simon (1947, 1955, 1959, 1976, 1978a,b) and later Heiner (1983, 1985) argued that human behaviour in a complex world could *only* be possible if the mind largely consisted of fairly simple rules operating on the information contained within the environment.

Definition 19 (Decision rules as algorithms). A decision rule is an algorithm, which is expressed mathematically as a recursive function $f_K(f_{K-1}(\ldots f_{K-K}(\cdot)))$ where each successive function $f_k(\cdot) \in \{f_k(\cdot)\}_{k=0}^{K}$ maps the outputs H_k of either the prior function $f_{k-1}(\cdot)$ or some basic information H_0 into the inputs H_{k+1} of either the next function $f_{k+1}(\cdot)$ in the recursion or some terminal information $H_{K+1} \in f_K(\cdot)$. That is $f_k(\cdot) : H_k \rightarrow H_{k+1} \forall k \in [1, \ldots, K]$.

The functions $f_k(\cdot)$ of which we here speak are the steps of an algorithmic chain which branch to one or the other answer to a question – the "if this, then that", "Yes/No", "True/False" statements of an algorithmic forward recursion. Each successive step answers a question posed of the outcome at the conclusion previous step. We can demonstrate these may be expressed both "long form" (the full algorithm) or as a particular iteration (the algorithm applied to perceptions $H' \subset \rho(v_N)$ of a particular set of information v_N) within mental networks or their application, respectively.

Theorem 5 ($g(H)$ may express decision rules). *Decision rules in long form,* $f_K (f_{K-1}(\ldots f_{K-K}(H_0)))$ *may be represented as chains of thought*

$$\left\{ \{h_k h_{k+1}\}_{h_k \in H_k} \right\}_{k=0}^{K} \subset g(H). \text{ Particular iterations of those rules } f_K(f_{K-1}(\ldots$$

$f_{K-K}(h_0 \in H_0)))$ *may be represented as single chains of thought* $\{h_k h_{k+1}\}_{k=0}^{K} \subset g(H')$, *provided that each "decision node" in the algorithm is perceived,* $\{h_k\}_{k=0}^{K+1} \subset H'$.

There was traditionally some controversy born of the analogy thus invited between mind and computer over whether the mind could process thoughts in parallel or but sequentially. John von Neumann (1958) was sceptical that the human brain (vicariously the mind) could process various analytical "tasks" in parallel in the manner a computer could by the simultaneous operation of its various "organs". On the other hand, the brain clearly has a number of different clusters of synaptic networks excited at any given time, which might suggest parallel processing in the mind. In the present formalism, parallel processing would exist when at least two analytical "tasks" $g \neq g'$ are executed within analysis $g(H')$ of a situation so that $g, g' \subset g(H')$. Nothing in our formalism prohibits this from being the case, similarly nothing requires it to be the case, leaving it to be a matter for empirical determination whether parallel processing is possible in the human mind as with a computer.

Any number of such rules (or "routines" as they came to be known in organisational psychology (Cyert and March, 1963; Nelson and Winter, 1982)) of any form might exist in the psyche. Particularly famous ones were proposed by Herbert Simon (1955) (the "satisficing – take the first acceptable" heuristic), by Reinhard Selten (1998, 1999) (the "meet aspirations adjusted for past performance" heuristic), by Amos Tversky (1972) (the "elimination by aspects" heuristic) and whoever it was that first proposed the "lexicographic" heuristic (Earl, 1990; Drakopoulos, 1994; Drakopoulos and Karayiannis, 2004). Gerd Gigerenzer (1999) imagines these all exist in an "adaptive toolbox" of "simple heuristics that make us smart", a set of rules which stand ready to guide our thinking and behaviour when called forth to analyse the environment. But how do such rules interact with preference to determine behaviour? We will return to this shortly to be more explicit about the origins of preference in general, but it is worth saying a little more given the traditional dissonance between the concepts of rules and preferences.

We might find that such rules in the psyche determine preferences "trivially", so that it is more accurate to say the individual is guided by the dictates of a *rule* than preference per se. Formally we could define such rule triviality with respect to particular rule $f_K(\cdot)$ as extant when an action being contained within the set $S[f_K(\cdot)]$ of actions which "satisfy" that rule,

$a \in S[f_K(\cdot)]$, implies a preference for that course of action over all others in the feasible set, that is,

$$a \in S[f_K(\cdot)] \Rightarrow g_a \succeq g_{a'} \, \forall a' \in B \tag{4.1}$$

which is to say that the behavioural rule "selects" a particular action out of feasible actions. However, this definition is a little too strong, for it implies that for any two feasible actions $a_i, a_i' \in B$ which are selected by the rule, a, $a' \in S[f_K(\cdot)]$ we would find that they have indifferent implications, $g_a \sim g_{a'}$[5]. A more satisfactory definition of rule-triviality is to define it in a proscriptory manner.

Definition 20 (Rule-triviality of $\succeq \circ 2^{g(H)}$). Preferences $\succeq \circ 2^{g(H)}$ are said to be rule-trivial with respect to a behavioural rule $f_K(\cdot)$ if the non-selection, $a' \notin S[f_K(\cdot)]$ of a certain action a' by that behavioural rule implies that it is *not* preferable to any action a which is so selected, $a \in S[f_K(\cdot)]$. That is, preferences $\succeq \circ 2^{g(H)}$ are rule-trivial with respect to $f_K(\cdot)$ if and only if

$$a' \notin S[f_K(\cdot)] \Rightarrow g_{a'} \not\succeq g_a \, \forall a \in f_K(\cdot) \tag{4.2}$$

We can see with this definition of rule-triviality of preferences how behaviour can be determined by rules, how "rule determinism" might exist if preferences are rule-trivial.

Theorem 6 (Rule-determinism in behaviour). *Suppose that preferences $\succeq$ $\circ 2^{g(H)}$ are rule-trivial with respect to $f_K(\cdot)$, that some action a is feasible ($a \in B$), is non-decomposable into any other feasible action (that is, $a \not\supset a' \forall a' \in B$) and has implications which are preference-comparable with all other feasible actions $a' \in B$ (that is, $g_a \succeq g_{a'}$, $g_{a'} \succeq g_a$ or both for all $a' \in B$). Then if a is the sole outcome which satisfies a behavioural rule $f_K(\cdot)$, $a = S[f_K(\cdot)]$, a will be selected by the individual, $a = a^*$.*

Note that if this is the case, we could not really say of behaviour that it is the outcome of rational deliberation over *ratio decidendi*. We would really have to say that the behaviour arises from the application of a rule, in all likelihood a very simple one (Heiner, 1983, 1985).

If Heiner (1983, 1985) is to be believed, and it is hard to refute him, then this rule-following rather than conscious "rational" deliberation is likely to inform the overwhelming majority of our behaviour. The world is simply too complex and our minds too limited to be thinking consciously about making complex value-judgements and constructing preferences on a regular basis. It is far better and "procedurally" rational for our preferences to be dictated, in the main, by the action of some set of simple rules upon our perception of the environment.

What we have discovered of the function of the brain and nervous system[6] would suggest, further, that the overwhelming majority of such rules operate in our subconscious. Thus a significant portion of our behaviour will be determined by mental processes beyond the realm of conscious awareness, and we may not even be aware of the processes by which our actions are determined. We will often behave without "thinking" about it consciously and, thanks to the influence of evolution on our mental networks (Edelman, 1987), still behave in such a particular, intricate and subtle manner as to function very effectively in the world. We may find that the "reasons" for why we acted a certain way only come "later", discovered by reflection on our environment, or created by rationalisation of rules operating deep within our subconscious and encoded deep within our brain.

In fact, we might even say that behaviour is the outcome of *habit*. Habits, in the pragmatic psychology of William James and John Dewey, are tendencies, proclivities toward a particular behaviour based in the individual's thought processes (Hodgson, 2010; Winter, 2013). That is precisely what rules of thought are here revealed to be. They are proclivities, tendencies toward a particular course of action. They will give rise to particular actions *if* the preferences they inform are rule-trivial and certain other technical conditions hold.

Rules, routines and habits of thought thus influence preference and behaviour, but they do not necessarily determine them. There may be more than one course of action selected by the rule. There may be more than one rule applicable to a particular situation, and they may "disagree" over what alternative ought be selected. In his very first formal paper on heuristic decision making Simon (1955) admitted that rules alone might not guarantee a unique solution to the problem of choice. The present formalism builds on and extends the heuristic cognitive psychology in resolving these problems. Decision rules play into the preferences $\succeq \circ 2^{g(H)}$ of the individual and may even determine them, but preferences must ultimately conform to equation 3.8, otherwise choice will not be well defined by the Make up Your Mind/Checkmate theorem (theorem 3). Where decision rules aren't sufficient to determine preferences $\succeq \circ 2^{g(H')}$, other considerations must act as a "tie-breaker" among competing considerations (Earl, 1983, 1986, 1990).

4.3 Reason and rules existing in dual-process psychology

We might think from the above that reasons and rules are dichotomous. Where one exists in mental networks the other does not. This is not so.

In fact there is a case to be made that reason and rules are two expressions for describing the same thing (Dopfer, 2004). But even aside from this, they might easily complement each other rather than contradict one another.

In the *Phaedrus* Plato makes an analogy of the human consciousness as a rider in a chariot endeavouring to coordinate two horses. One representing "goodness" and "beauty" in the human soul and the other the other aspects of the human soul. Recalling that for Socratic philosophy, "goodness" and "beauty" are synonymic for "reason", and *doxa* (the lowest form of knowledge for the Platonic Socratics in particular and root of the word "orthodoxy") is a form of base rule following we might rename the two horses "reason" and "rules". An apt analogy, for if the horses pull in opposite directions – work at cross-purposes – the chariot will slow to the point of stasis. If they work as a (literal) team, pulling in the same direction, the chariot will fly forward at pace. This duality recurs over and over throughout psychology.

Herbert Simon (1976, 1978a,b) speaks of two types of rationality. "Procedural" rationality is applying rules and procedures which facilitate quick and effective determination of preference, avoiding the irrationality of a paralysing comparison of pros and cons. "Substantive" rationality consists of deliberation over what actions will attain certain objectives. The two work in concert, balancing and feeding back one to the other. Heiner (1983, 1985) demonstrated this formally, arguing the gap between psychological capability and the demands of the environment makes rule-following a much "better bet" in making the right decision, especially if combined with reasoning when decisions are consistently found to be "wrong". Leibenstein (1976) proposes rationality is "selective", the consciousness deems whether or not a situation demands the engaging in rational processes of thought rather than simple rule-following. A neuroscientific basis has been discovered in "controlled" process of thought directed by conscious deliberation, and "automated" processes animated by simple brain function (Camerer et al., 2005). And of course, Kahneman (2003) rediscovered Simon's dual process theory in his distinction between thought in system 1 (fast, reactive, rule based) and system 2 (slow, deliberative, purposive).

In the present formalism we have rule-based cognitive psychology accommodated through their expression in mental networks $\mu = \{H \quad g(H)\}$ of decision rules (definition 19, theorem 5). We have the concept of thought reasoning accommodated through their expression in mental networks $\mu = \{H \quad g(H)\}$ of sentence-equivalents (definition 18, theorem 4). The two may, must, coexist. It is difficult to imagine an individual who never uses a simple "rule of thumb" to guide their decisions, and it is difficult, impossible in fact, to imagine of ourselves reading this text without some form of language being "spoken" in our minds.

Both reasoning and rule-following inform preferences $\succeq o2^{g(H)}$. They may all "agree" in the direction they give to $\succeq o2^{g(H)}$, but they may also be so variegated in the direction they give that they may lead to a failure of the necessary conditions of the "make up your mind/checkmate" theorem (3). If they disagree, but are not so variegated, the individual might be able to impose some form of mediation, a "constitution" of sorts which overrides the one or the other tendency by recourse to some higher "court" in the consciousness or rule system (Earl, 1986) – Sen (1977, pp. 337–341) speaks of a "meta-preference" to decide, for instance, when sympathetic tendencies compete with the selfish. If the reason and rules "pull" in roughly the same direction, the individual can discover the best course of action their construction of reality is revealing to them. If they "pull" in opposite directions, the rider can never hope to discover it, and will be paralysed by indecision.

4.4 Social factors in the psychological process

The individual here is much more a point around which we pivot in understanding how their environment maps into their behaviour than an isolated "atom" (Lawson, 2006, 2013; Hodgson, 2007). In fact, the environment is equally primitive to the theory as is the individual. The individual is *not* isolated from the world in any sense, the whole point is to understand how they interact with it. The whole point of perception is to provide the interface between the world and the individual's personal vision, personal knowledge of it (Merleau-Ponty, 1945, 1948; Polanyi, 1958).

The environment of the individual, v_N, must by rights contain their neighbourhood within what Habermas (1962) called the "public sphere" as well as the "private sphere". These spheres are the medium in which all our social interaction takes place. In the ancient world these were limited to home, street and *agora*, or *forum* (the public square). Now they are everywhere aided by modern communication technology. Our social life consists of interacting with each other in these spheres, our psychological process mediating between the social world and social behaviour (Schutz, 1932).

In social environments, our psychological process mediates between the world and our behaviour, guiding thinking about how and why to act through the process of perception, analysis and decision. One interpretation of this, as we have seen, is as a process of *reasoning*. Margaret Archer (2003) calls this the process of the "internal conversation", the process whereby the individual "talks through" their thoughts. In our language here, the individual constructs sentence equivalents in their minds, connecting the various objects and events in their environment to make sense of society. Social Exchange

Theory (Knox, 1963; Emerson, 1976) sees society as emergent from such processes of "reasoning" about the most preferable manner in which to act in society, as does what has been called the "New Institutional Economics" (Williamson, 1975, 1979, 1985, 2002; Ostrom, 1990, 2000; Ostrom and Basurto, 2011; North, 1990, 1991; Coase, 1937, 1984).

Another interpretation, which has been more the tendency of sociology (again, see Archer, 2003), is to see individuals' thinking about their social environment as a process of applying *rules* of one form or another. Seabright (2004) has argued compellingly for this vision by noting that it is cognitively and technologically impossible to mould environments so as to enforce the adherence we observe to social norms by inducement and incentive alone. Rules *must* assume a significant position in the government of social behaviour.

If preferences are rule-trivial, and the rules applied to think about a social environment are social rules, then social behaviour will not so much be guided by "rational" thought as by the dictates of social rules. This is the psychological process underlying what might be called the "French" anthropological sociology, the "American" institutional sociology and the "Cambridge" social ontology.

Once we realise, as Dopfer (2004) does, that rules guide *thinking* as much as they guide behaviour, we recognise that social rules contained in our mental networks are the expression of what Bourdieu (1972, 1980) called *habitus. Habitus* is the total of our habituated thought inherited from our society's culture, and is the expression of our practical ethics. *Habitus* guides our thinking about how and why to act in society, it influences our behaviour and is an architecture of rules in our psyche. Michel de Certeau (1984) makes an analogy between this rule structure in the psyche and the rules by which we read a text to extract meaning, and write a text to express meaning. The text is society, the rules for understanding it and adding to it our *habitus*, our system of rules for thinking and acting. Michel de Certeau (1984) is subversive relative to Bourdieu (1972, 1980), and also recognises how we are not merely the totality of social rules because within each individual mind is variation on the rules for interpreting the social world, thinking about it and acting in it, so that our individuality is maintained alongside cultural identity.

The Cambridge Social Ontologists, and their chief interlocutor John Searle (2010), offer a specific form for the rules which give rise to social action. They say that social rules are institutions, which are a connective structure between people, situations, social position and rights, obligations and empowerments. Specifically institutions are rules of a form "in situation i, j occupies social k which is associated with rights r, obligations o and empowerments e". Searle (2010) has a legalistic view of their origin in statements which are both expressive and declarative, much as Hart (1961) viewed the law. Tony Lawson (2003, 2009, 2012, 2015a,b,c) and the Cambridge social ontologists (see Arena and Lawson, 2015, and Faulkner et al., 2017) see the social positions k as emergent from an evolutionary process. These rules are expressed in the individual psyche and serve to orient the individual to the social world, to allow them to interpret it, their place, and their role within it, and guide their actions accordingly.

The "American" (though now more European) institutional sociology originates in the works of Veblen (1899, 1904, 1914) especially and his followers Hamilton (1919), Mitchell (1913), Ayres (1953) and Commons (1924, 1931, 1934) (Hodgson, 2004; Hodgson and Knudsen, 2010), who saw human interaction in society as intermediated by social institutions, rules which individuals would apply to make sense of their environment and how to act in it. Whispers of this theory infuse the work of Erving Goffman (1956) who draws parallels between the rules of social action and the playing of a part in a theatre production. The institutional theory of social interaction draws heavily on pragmatic psychology to establish an influence for institutions over the psyche (Hodgson, 2010; Winter, 2013). Habits are proclivities toward certain patterns of thought and behaviour, tendencies to behave in a certain way based on patterns of thought. In our language, they are rules for thinking and behaviour, establishing connections between objects and events which create a proclivity toward a particular social behaviour, and guide social behaviour if they have a sufficient hold over preference.

This theory we have offered of the psychological process is therefore not one of an isolated individual. The individual exists in an environment which contains the private and public spheres of society, they think about the social environment either by reason or by applying rules, and from that thinking about their place and role in the social world emerges their action in society. Expanding on the origins of ideas which become reasons and rules for interpreting society and how to act in it, and expanding on the outcomes in systems of human interaction of such actions, is a major direction, perhaps even the most important direction for coming research in the Science of Everyday Life.

4.5 Motivation theory, the theory of value judgments and the origins of preference

In developing our theory of the psychological process we have hitherto remained somewhat obscure about the origins of the aesthetics which give rise to the preference structure $\succeq \circ 2^{g(H)}$ defined on subsets of individual thought $2^{g(H)}$. We have said only that it is implied by the language in which personal knowledge $g(H)$ is expressed. Having now given greater consideration to how the mental network $\mu = \{H \ \ g(H)\}$ and its application to any given environment, $g(H') \subset g(H)$ is to be interpreted, we are in a better position to expand the theory of the origin of preferences $\succeq \circ 2^{g(H)}$ defined on subsets of individual thought.

The chains $g_a \subset g(H')$ which comprise either reasoning or the application of rules to assessing a particular course of action a seem to lend themselves toward the interpretation of having terminal points than being circular logics. Such an interpretation would suggest that such points, we might call them $\psi \subset H$, exist "deeper" toward the "core" of the psyche, following from particular courses of action and extending through mental networks $\mu = \{H \ \ g(H)\}$ as they do. These points serve to "anchor" chains of thought (Kelly, 1963; Hinkle, 1965) as would the logical axioms of a chain of reasoning or "stop points" of the operation of an algorithm. The first axiom of drive theory then hypothesises that these points $\psi \subset H$ in the "deep" psyche might give rise to the aesthetics which manifest as preferences.

Definition 21 (First axiom of the origins of preference). The complexes $g_\psi \subset g(H)$ which connect various points ψ of the "deep" psyche give rise to the aesthetics which manifest as the preferences $\succeq \circ 2^{g(H)}$ defined on subsets of individual thought $2^{g(H)}$. That is,

$$g_\psi \subset g(H) \Rightarrow \succeq \circ 2^{g(H)} \tag{4.3}$$

Various interpretations may be offered of the complexes g_ψ which connect elements of the "deep" psyche ψ drawing on various motivational theories and theories of value judgments, which thereby integrates those theories into the present theory of the psychological process.

If we were to interpret mental networks $\mu = \{H \ \ g(H)\}$ as expressing algorithmic rule structures, then we may interpret the complexes g_ψ connecting elements of the "deep" psyche ψ according to the cognitive theory of Herbert Simon (1967). This theory is that the complexes g_ψ are comprised of the final steps in algorithmic behavioural rules. The termini, ψ, are to be understood in this theory to be "controls" on the cognitive processes provided by behavioural "drives" – need, want and emotion. Once a particular need, want or emotion is known to be satiated or elicited by some course of action, preference might be determined between its outcomes and those expected of another.

The quasi-cognitive theory of personal construct psychology (Kelly, 1963; Hinkle, 1965) offers an analogous interpretation of the complexes

g_ψ connecting elements of the "deep" psyche ψ. George Kelly and especially his student Hinkle theorised that personal constructs are organised hierarchically in such a fashion that thoughts, when filtered through personal constructs, arrive at axiomatic endpoints. The complexes g_ψ connecting elements of the "deep" psyche ψ thus position the ultimate outputs of reasoning about various courses of action relative to the "axes" provided by the elements of the "deep"psyche ψ. These complexes thus provide an axiomatic foundation, if you like, for a practical ethics.

If we were to interpret the mental networks $\mu = \{H \quad g(H)\}$ as expressing *ratio decidendi* our interpretations of the complexes g_ψ connecting elements of the "deep" psyche ψ would move into more psychoanalytic realms. In Maslow's theory (Maslow, 1943, 1954), the terminal elements of chains of reason in the "deep" psyche ψ are needs and wants, behavioural "drives" which the complexes g_ψ position courses of action relative to. But the complexes g_ψ connecting elements of the "deep" psyche ψ contain also a hierarchical relation (to which we will return) between those motivational elements of the "deep" psyche which affect the preferences $\succeq o2^{g(H)}$ that arise from them.

In Freud's theory (Freud, 1917, 1930, 1963), an exciting and dynamic one, the complexes g_ψ connecting elements of the "deep" psyche ψ become the expressions of a battle between competing sets (Lester, 1995) of desires contained within the subconscious, quasi-barbaric "Id" and the inhibitory, socially constructed "Superego" mediated by the conscious "Ego".[7] As the "Id" and "Superego" desires within the "deep" psyche ψ gain the "upper hand" in the complexes g_ψ come to dominate analysis $g(H')$ of the environment $v_N : \rho (v_N) \supset H'$, so too do their demands shape preferences $\succeq o2^{g(H)}$ on subsets of thought, the feeling attached to those thoughts.

Most profound of all interpretations of the complexes g_ψ connecting elements of the "deep" psyche ψ is that offered by Carl Jung (Jung, 1933, 1935, 1964). In his theory, the complexes g_ψ connecting elements of the "deep" psyche ψ take the form of the mysterious but potent "Archetype", sitting deep within the psyche in both the tacit dimension (Polanyi, 1967) of which we cannot speak but by analogy and symbol, and the unconscious. Archetypes force themselves into the consciousness in dreams especially (Jung, 1933, 1935, 1964, 1974) where they can by their nature only be described by allusion and symbol, being of a pre-linguistic origin in the collective unconscious. Jung theorised they became manifest in myth and religion by storytelling (Jung, 1933, 1935, 1964; Campbell, 1972; Campbell and Moyers, 1988), so it is no accident that as such, myth and religion contain ethical teaching and symbols of morality. They are practical ethics, ethical speeches seeking to move *ethos* in the human spirit as Aristotle would have said, because that is what the Archetype is, a moral core upon which practical ethics are constructed. The archetypes of the collective unconscious are the organising principle upon which personal knowledge of the world is predicated (Polanyi, 1958). Sitting deep in the psyche and influencing the whole of thought about how and why to act in the world expressed in mental networks μ = $\{H \quad g(H)\}$ which are organised around them, the Archetypes as complexes g_ψ connecting elements of the "deep" psyche ψ connecting deep moral and ethical elements of the psyche are the origins of our sense of value. They endow us with the ability to discriminate on the basis of value and thus inform the aesthetics attached to various subsets of thought $2^{g(H)}$, and therefore allow us to make *value judgments* which manifest in our preferences $\succeq$ $\circ 2^{g(H)}$ over subsets of thought.

These theories which interpret the nature of the complexes g_ψ connecting elements of the "deep" psyche ψ together and the manner of their influence on preferences $\succeq \circ 2^{g(H)}$ suggest a second axiom for the theory of the origins of preference which goes beyond the first. They suggest that these complexes g_ψ are not merely sufficient for aesthetics, value judgments and preferences to exist, but are also *necessary*. Thus the second axiom of the theory of the origin of preferences.

Definition 22 (Second axiom of the origins of preference). A preference relation $\succeq$ may be established between two subsets of thought g, $g' \subset g(H)$ only if they intersect with the complexes g_ψ connecting elements of the "deep" psyche ψ. That is,

$$g \succsim g' \vee g' \succsim g \vee g \sim g' \Rightarrow g \cap g_\psi \neq \emptyset \ \& \ g' \cap g_\psi \neq \emptyset \quad (4.4)$$

The implications of this axiom in the context of our theory of the psychological process are particularly interesting.

Theorem 7 (The consequences of nihilism). *If the second axiom of the theory of the origins of preference (definition 22) holds, then the individual may only decide to act if the implications g_a of each and every feasible course of action $a \in B$ overlap with the complexes g_ψ connecting elements of the "deep" psyche ψ. That is,*

$$\exists a = a^* \Rightarrow g_a \cap g_\psi \neq \emptyset \ \forall a \in B \quad (4.5)$$

In other words, under what we might call "drive theory", *everyone* must have an active moral core and practical ethics. Everyone must be able to discriminate on the basis of value and make value judgments. Some form of morality and ethics, some form of value structure is *necessary* for us to function in the world. We cannot be nihilists and still function. We *require* a system which allows us to discriminate on the basis of value, we *must* have a system which gives rise to our aesthetics. Without such a system, a moral and practical core, a system for discriminating on the basis of value we cannot act in the world. Without a moral core around which our ethics are organised, by which we make value judgments, we are paralysed.

Notes

1. This is a conception of rational thought far more consistent with the notion of rationality as reason widely accepted in philosophy and law than the unusual definition given to it by economists as a decision rule supported by a pre-ordering of available actions which is complete (every single action can be ranked against every other) and transitive (if three actions are ranked a_1 to a_2 and a_2 to a_3, then a_1 is ranked to a_3) (Debreu, 1959; Mas-Collel et al., 1995; Rubinstein, 2006; Jehle and Reny, 2011). That is really no more "rational" than picking at random, there is no "reason" for the choice but for the assertion "because it is preferred". Really it is rather *irrational*, there is no consideration of the consequences of the act beyond preference, there is certainly no proposition to be tested against reality. On notions of reason and rationality see Jon Elster (2009).
2. Further developed at some great length in Newell et al. (1958, 1962), Newell and Simon (1972), and Newell (1990) as well as Simon (1998).
3. A number of cognitive scientists such as Pinker (1998) and Duncan (2010) go further to say that the mind *is* a computer, not merely analogous. It is a different kind of computer than the eponymous machines we use, but insofar as it processes information by applying certain rules, it is a computational system.
4. Mie Augier (2001) notes that this isomorphism between the mind and the computer was what led Herbert Simon to enter the field of computer science and make seminal contributions therein approaching the significance of those of Alan Turing himself.
5. Since we would have, by this criterion, $g_a \succeq g_{a'}$ and $g_{a'} \succeq g_a$.
6. For instance, just how little the cerebral cortex, where "higher" cognitive functions are encoded, is often involved in behaviour relative to the amygdala, hypothalamus and cerebellum (Kandel et al., 2013).
7. The concept of the Superego would, however, not emerge until Freud's later writings (see Freud, 1930, and 1963). It is conflated with a part of the Ego in *A General Introduction to Psychoanalysis* (1917).

References

Archer, M., 2003. *Structure, Agency and the Internal Conversation*. Cambridge University Press, Cambridge.

Arena, R., Lawson, T., 2015. Introduction (special issue: Contributions to the history of ontological thinking in economics, with a specific focus on "process and order"). *Cambridge Journal of Economics* 39, 987–992.

Augier, M., 2001. Sublime Simon: The consistent vision of economic psychology's Nobel laureate. *Journal of Economic Psychology* 22, 307–334.

Ayer, A., 1936. *Language, Truth and Logic.* Penguin, London.

Ayres, C., 1953. The role of technology in economic theory. *American Economic Review* 43 (2), 279–287.

Bourdieu, P., 1972. *Outline of a Theory of Practice.* Cambridge University Press, Cambridge.

Bourdieu, P., 1980. *The Logic of Practice.* Polity Press, Cambridge.

Camerer, C., Loewenstein, G., Prelec, D., 2005. Neuroeconomics: How neuroscience can inform economics. *Journal of Economic Literature* XLIII, 9–64.

Campbell, J., 1972. *Myths to Live By.* Penguin, London.

Campbell, J., Moyers, B., 1988. *The Power of Myth.* Anchor Books, New York.

Coase, R., 1937. The nature of the firm. *Economica* (New Series) 4 (6), 386–405.

Coase, R., 1984. The new institutional economics. *Journal of Institutional and Theoretical Economics* 140, 229–231.

Commons, J., 1924. *Legal Foundations of Capitalism.* The MacMillan Company, New York.

Commons, J., 1931. Institutional economics. *American Economic Review* 21 (4), 648–657.

Commons, J., 1934. *Institutional Economics.* MacMillan, New York.

Cyert, R., March, J., 1963. *A Behavioral Theory of the Firm.* Prentice-Hall, Inc., Englewood Cliffs.

de Certeau, M., 1984. *The Practice of Everyday Life.* University of California Press, Berkeley.

Debreu, G., 1959. *The Theory of Value.* Cowles Foundation Monographs. Yale University Press, New Haven.

Dopfer, K., 2004. The economic agent as rule marker and rule user: Homo sapiens oeconomicus. *Journal of Evolutionary Economics* 14, 177–195.

Drakopoulos, S., 1994. Hierarchical choice in economics. *Journal of Economic Surveys* 8 (2), 133–153.

Drakopoulos, S., Karayiannis, A., 2004. The historical development of hierarchical behavior in economic thought. *Journal of the History of Economic Thought* 26 (3), 363–378.

Duncan, J., 2010. *How Intelligence Happens.* Yale University Press, New Haven.

Earl, P., 1983. *The Economic Imagination.* Wheatsheaf, Brighton.

Earl, P., 1986. *Lifestyle Economics.* Harvester Wheatsheaf, Brighton.

Earl, P., 1990. Economics and psychology: A survey. *Economic Journal* 100 (402), 718–755.

Edelman, G., 1987. *Neural Darwinism.* Basic Books, New York.

Elster, J., 2009. *Reason and Rationality.* Princeton University Press, Princeton.

Emerson, R., 1976. Social exchange theory. *Annual Review of Sociology* 2, 335–362.

Faulkner, P., Pratten, S., Runde, J., 2017. Cambridge social ontology: Clarification, development and deployment. *Cambridge Journal of Economics* 41 (5), 1265–1277.

Freud, S., 1917. *A General Introduction to Psychoanalysis.* Wordsworth Editions, Hertfordshire.

Freud, S., 1930. *Civilisation and Its Discontents.* Penguin, London.

Freud, S., 1963. *Therapy and Technique.* Collier, New York.

Gigerenzer, G., 1999. *Bounded Rationality.* Dahlem Workshop Reports. MIT Press, Cambridge, MA, Ch. The adaptive toolbox, pp. 37–50.

Goffman, E., 1956. *The Presentation of Self in Everyday Life*. Penguin, New York.

Habermas, J., 1962. *The Structural Transformation of the Public Sphere*. Polity, Cambridge.

Hamilton, W., 1919. The institutional approach to economic theory. *American Economic Review* 9 (1), 309–318.

Hart, H., 1961. *The Concept of Law*. Oxford University Press, Oxford.

Heiner, R., 1983. The origin of predictable behavior. *American Economic Review* 73 (4), 560–595.

Heiner, R., 1985. Origin of predictable behavior: Further modelling and applications. *American Economic Review* 75 (2), 391–396.

Hinkle, D., 1965. *The Change of Personal Constructs From the Viewpoint of a Theory of Construct Implications*. Doctoral dissertation, Ohio State University.

Hodgson, G., 2004. *The Evolution of Institutional Economics*. Routledge, London.

Hodgson, G., 2007. Meanings of methodological individualism. *Journal of Economic Methodology* 14 (2), 211–226.

Hodgson, G., 2010. Choice, habit and evolution. *Journal of Evolutionary Economics* 20, 1–18.

Hodgson, G., Knudsen, T., 2010. *Darwin's Conjecture*. University of Chicago Press, Chicago.

Jehle, A., Reny, P., 2011. *Advanced Microeconomic Theory*. Prentice Hall/Financial Times, London.

Jung, C., 1933. *Modern Man in Search of a Soul*. Routledge, London.

Jung, C., 1935. *Analytical Psychology*. Routledge, London.

Jung, C. (Ed.), 1964. *Man and His Symbols*. Bantam Doubleday Dell, New York.

Jung, G., 1974. *Dreams*. Routledge, London.

Kahneman, D., 2003. Maps of bounded rationality: Psychology for behavioural economics. *American Economic Review* 93 (5), 1449–1475.

Kandel, E., Schwartz, J., Jessell, T., Siegelbaum, S., Hudspeth, A. (Eds.), 2013. *Principles of Neural Science*, 5th Edition. McGraw-Hill, New York.

Kelly, G., 1963. *A Theory of Personality*. Norton, New York.

Knox, J., 1963. The concept of exchange in sociological theory: 1884 and 1961. *Social Forces* 41 (4), 341–346.

Lawson, T., 2003. *Re-orienting Economics*. Routledge, London.

Lawson, T., 2006. The nature of heterodox economics. *Cambridge Journal of Economics* 30, 483–505.

Lawson, T., 2009. Cambridge social ontology: An interview with Tony Lawson. *Erasmus Journal for Philosophy and Economics* 2 (1), 100–122.

Lawson, T., 2012. Ontology and the study of social reality: Emergence, organisation, community, power, social relations, corporations, artefacts and money. *Cambridge Journal of Economics* 36, 345–385.

Lawson, T., 2013. What is this "school" called neoclassical economics? *Cambridge Journal of Economics* 37, 947–983.

Lawson, T., 2015a. Comparing conceptions of social ontology: Emergent social entities and/or institutional facts? *Cambridge Working Papers in Economics*, No. 1514.

Lawson, T., 2015b. The nature of the firm and the peculiarities of the corporation. *Cambridge Journal of Economics* 39, 1–32.

Lawson, T., 2015c. Process, order and stability in Veblen. *Cambridge Journal of Economics* 39, 993–1030.

56   *Reasons, rules, society and motivation*

Leibenstein, H., 1976. *Beyond Economic Man*. Harvard University Press, Cambridge, MA.
Lester, D., 1995. *Theories of Personality*. Taylor & Francis, Washington.
Mas-Collel, A., Winston, M., Green, J., 1995. *Microeconomic Theory*. Oxford University Press, Oxford.
Maslow, A., 1943. A theory of human motivation. *Psychological Review* 50 (4), 370–396.
Maslow, A., 1954. *Motivation and Personality*. Harper & Brothers, New York.
Merleau-Ponty, M., 1945. *Phenomenology of Perception*. Routledge, London.
Merleau-Ponty, M., 1948. *The World of Perception*. Routledge, London.
Mitchell, W., 1913. *Business Cycles*. University of California Press, Berkeley.
Nelson, R., Winter, S., 1982. *An Evolutionary Theory of Economic Change*. Belknap Harvard University Press, Cambridge, MA.
Newell, A., 1990. *Unified Theories of Cognition*. Harvard University Press, Cambridge, MA.
Newell, A., Shaw, J., Simon, H., 1958. Elements of a theory of human problem solving. *Psychological Review* 65 (3), 151–166.
Newell, A., Shaw, J., Simon, H., 1962. *Contemporary Approaches to Creative Thinking*. Behavioral Science Series. Atherton Press, New York, Ch. The processes of creative thinking, pp. 63–119.
Newell, A., Simon, H., 1972. *Human Problem Solving*. Prentice Hall, Englewood Cliffs.
North, D., 1990. *Institutions, Institutional Change and Economic Performance*. Cambridge University Press, Cambridge.
North, D., 1991. Institutions. *Journal of Economic Perspectives* 5 (1), 97–112.
Ostrom, E., 1990. *Governing the Commons*. Cambridge University Press, Cambridge.
Ostrom, E., 2000. Collective action and the evolution of social norms. *The Journal of Economic Perspectives* 14 (3), pp. 137–158.
Ostrom, E., Basurto, X., 2011. Crafting analytical tools to study institutional change. *Journal of Institutional Economics* 7 (3), 317–343.
Pears, D., 1971. *Wittgenstein. Fontana Modern Masters*. Fontana, New York.
Pinker, S., 1998. *How the Mind Works*. Penguin, London.
Polanyi, M., 1958. *Personal Knowledge*. Routledge and Kegan Paul, London.
Polanyi, M., 1967. *The Tacit Dimension*. Routledge and Kegan Paul, London.
Popper, K., 1934. *Logic of Scientific Discovery*. Routledge, London.
Rubinstein, A., 2006. *Lecture Notes in Microeconomic Theory*. Princeton University Press, Princeton.
Schutz, A., 1932. *The Phenomenology of the Social World*. Northwestern University Press, Evanston.
Seabright, P., 2004. *The Company of Strangers*. Princeton University Press, Princeton.
Searle, J., 2010. *Making the Social World*. Oxford University Press, Oxford.
Selten, R., 1998. Aspiration adaptation theory. *Journal of Mathematical Psychology* 42, 191–214.
Selten, R., 1999. *Bounded Rationality*. Dahlem Workshop Reports. MIT Press, Cambridge, MA, Ch. What is bounded rationality? pp. 13–36.
Sen, A., 1977. Rational fools: A critique of the behavioural foundations of economic theory. *Philosophy and Public Affairs* 6 (4), 317–344.
Simon, H., 1947. *Administrative Behavior*, 4th Edition. The Free Press, New York.

Simon, H., 1955. A behavioural model of rational choice. *Quarterly Journal of Economics* 69 (1), 99–118.

Simon, H., 1956. Rational choice and the structure of the environment. *Psychological Review* 63 (2), 129–138.

Simon, H., 1959. Theories of decision-making in economics and behavioural science. *American Economic Review* 49 (3), 3.

Simon, H., 1967. Motivation and emotional controls of cognition. *Psychological Review* 74 (1), 29–39.

Simon, H., 1969. *The Sciences of the Artificial*. MIT Press, Cambridge, MA.

Simon, H., 1976. *Method and Appraisal in Economics*. Cambridge University Press, Cambridge, Ch. From substantive to procedural rationality, pp. 129–148.

Simon, H., 1978a. On how to decide what to do. *Bell Journal of Economics* 9 (2), 494–507.

Simon, H., 1978b. Rationality as a process and as product of thought. *American Economic Review* 68 (2), 1–16.

Simon, H., 1998. Discovering explanations. *Minds and Machines* 8, 7–37.

Turing, A., 1950. Computing machinery and intelligence. *Mind* LIX (236), 433–460.

Tversky, A., 1972. Elimination by aspects: A theory of choice. *Psychological Review* 79 (4), 281–299.

Veblen, T., 1899. *The Theory of the Leisure Class*. Oxford University Press, Oxford World's Classics.

Veblen, T., 1904. *The Theory of Business Enterprise*. Charles Scribners, New York.

Veblen, T., 1914. *The Instinct of Workmanship, and the State of the Industrial Arts*. MacMillan, New York.

von Neumann, J., 1958. *The Computer and the Brain*. Yale University Press, New Haven.

Williamson, O., 1975. *Markets and Hierarchies*. The Free Press, New York.

Williamson, O., 1979. Transaction-cost economics: The governance of contract relations. *Journal of Law and Economics* XXII (2), 233–261.

Williamson, O., 1985. *The Economic Institutions of Capitalism*. Free Press, New York.

Williamson, O., 2002. The theory of the firm as governance structure: From choice to contract. *Journal of Economic Perspectives* 16 (3), 171–195.

Winter, S., 2013. Habit, deliberation, and action: Strengthening the microfoundations of routines and capabilities. *The Academy of Management Perspectives* 27 (2), 120–137.

Wittgenstein, L., 1914–1916. *Notebooks, 1914–1916*, 2nd Edition. University of Chicago Press, Chicago.

Wittgenstein, L., 1921. *Tractatus Logico-Philosophicus*. Routledge, London.

Wittgenstein, L., 1953. *Philosophical Investigations*, 4th Edition. Wiley-Blackwell, Chicester.

Wittgenstein, L., King, J., Lee, D., 1930–1932. *Wittgenstein's Lectures: Cambridge 1930–1932*. Rowman & Littlefield, Lanham.

5 Substitutability and behavioural change in quasi-fixed environments

Considering now the dynamics of behaviour, it will be interesting to consider a factor in the psyche which is of some significance in quasi-fixed environments, where but a few bits of information are subject to variation.[1] This factor is the state of substitutability between different courses of action which has been all but universally assumed at the core of traditional and operational models of economic behaviour (Earl, 1986a; Drakopoulos, 1994; Drakopoulos and Karayiannis, 2004). Substitutability is essential in such environments for inducing behavioural change through the manipulation of "tradeoffs", or what economists like to call "incentives". Non-substitutability on the other hand allows us to make sense of the constraints in the *psyche* on the ability to induce behavioural change in quasi-fixed environments. Non-substitutability allows us to understand when the individual *cannot* be induced to engage in certain behaviours and why more wholesale changes to the environment and psyche might be necessary.

First, we shall consider substitutability, define how in the psyche it serves to relate courses of action to each other and elaborate how this impacts behaviour. We will then consider how this informs us about "basic" non-substitutability, about which heuristic theory in cognitive psychology may inform us. A much "deeper", more "fundamental" non-substitutability shall then be considered which owes its existence to the distinction of need from want, and the basic constraints it places on behaviour. The final portion of the spectrum of behaviour we shall consider pertains to the polar contrary of substitutability – complementarity.

5.1 Substitutability: "I'll take it, eventually"

Substitutability between two courses of action can be said to exist when the one may be substituted for the other with roughly equivalent outcomes in terms of preferability.

Definition 23 (Substitutability). A course of action a can be said to be substitutable for another course of action a' if and only if the implications of choosing a are approximately equivalent those of choosing a', that is, if and only if

$$g_a \sim g_{a'} \qquad\qquad (5.1)$$

We can show the effect this has on behaviour in the following result.

Theorem 8 (Substitutability causes behavioural change). *Take two actions a,a' and suppose initially that the latter is selected $a' = a^*$. Suppose further that there is a descriptor δ which can be attached to a in the implications $g_a \subset g(H')$, as well as the following technical conditions:*

1 *There is a sequence of such descriptors $\{\delta_\theta\}_{\theta=0}^{\Theta}$ for which the implications associated with a' and δ_θ remain preference-comparable but non-decreasing in terms of preference across the sequence $\theta \in [0,\ldots,\Theta]$. That is, $g_a^{\delta_\theta} \npreceq g_a^{\delta_{\theta'}} \Leftrightarrow \theta > \theta'$.*
2 *The preference structure $\succeq o2^{g(H)}$ is transitive with respect to rankings of the implications of the two actions a and a' and any other particular action a''.*
3 *The implications of the course of action a maintain their preference relation to those of any other $a'' \in B$. That is, $g_a \succeq g_{a''}\forall a'' \in B$.*

If the point at which the former course of action a becomes substitutable for the other a' occurs at some descriptor $\delta_{\bar\theta} : \bar\theta < \Theta$ then the prevailing of some descriptor $\delta_\theta : \theta > \bar\theta$ will cause a change of behaviour $a' = a^* \to a = a^*$.

This theorem illustrates the manner in which substitutability facilitates behavioural change in quasi-fixed environments. If a point exists at which

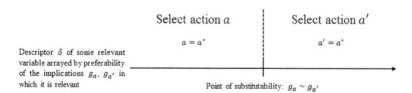

Figure 5.1 Inducing behavioural change in quasi-fixed environments: as long as a state of substitutability exists (and some other technical conditions are satisfied), then changing some incentive sufficiently (for instance, making it so that we move from left to right along the "descriptor" axis above) will induce a change of behaviour.

some variable δ induces substitutability between the outcomes of two courses of action, so too will there be substitution between those courses of action, those behaviours. It illustrates that where substitutability exists, some variable δ can be "traded off" against to the point at which the tradeoffs will cause a change of behaviour. If substitutability exists, thoughts about courses of action will be of a "I'll take it eventually" nature, the "it" being some course of action and the "eventually" referring to the variable which if changed sufficiently will induce substitutability and thus substitution between courses of action. There is some "mix" of incentives which can induce the selecting of one course of action over another.

As Earl (1983) put it well, in this context the individual is "up for anything". they can be induced to engage in any behaviour given the "right mix" of tradeoffs if a point of substitutability exists. Neoclassical economics, especially that of Alfred Marshall (1890) offers a good model of such behaviour. When substitutability exists, the individual is trading off "costs" against "benefits". They will continue to hold to some behaviour until the marginal cost of that behaviour exceeds the marginal benefit, at which point they will have reached a state of substitutability and may switch to some other course of action. To induce a change of behaviour then, all one needs to do is get the "price" right, the right mix of incentives.

5.2   Non-substitutability: "It just doesn't Cut It"

The most basic form of non-substitutability is simply that, the negation of substitutability. It exists whenever we one course of action *cannot* be substituted for the other with roughly equivalent outcomes in terms of preferability.

Figure 5.2 The limits to inducement and incentive: fantastic deals and tempting for some, but being a man I wouldn't take them even if they were free.

Definition 24 (Non-substitutability). A course of action a can be said to be non-substitutable for another course of action a' if and only if the implications of choosing the one a are not approximately equivalent those of choosing the other a', that is, if and only if

$$g_a \not\approx g_{a'} \tag{5.2}$$

By reference to theorem 8, non-substitutability manifests as there *not* being a descriptor δ that can be attached to a course of action a by the implications $g_a \subset g(H')$ in a sequence $\{\delta_\theta\}_{\theta=0}^{\Theta}$ at which it becomes substitutable for some other, a'.[2] There would then be no way to induce the selection of a by variation of δ, having the individual trade the outcomes g_a that induces relative to $g_{a'}$ until a' can be substituted for a.

It seems ridiculous to those of us with a traditional training in economic theory to suppose that individuals may regularly not make trade-offs between the outcomes of various courses of action available to them such that they would be willing to engage in *any* kind of behaviour if only the right mix of outcomes could be found. That is what we assume behaviour to be constituted by, any other behaviour runs counter to the "Archimedean" axiom lying at the core of traditional and operational economic theory (Earl, 1983; Drakopoulos, 1994; Drakopoulos and Karayiannis, 2004). Human behaviour is however, in the main, not driven by trade-offs of this outcome against that, not of the "I'll take it, eventually" nature, it is instead driven by *cut-offs*, it is of the "it just doesn't Cut It" nature, the "it" being some course of action, and "doesn't Cut It" referring to situational requirements which a course of action either can meet or cannot.

This realisation is central to heuristic cognitive psychology. In the very first paper on the subject, Simon (1955) speaks about satisfaction levels which an action *must* meet before it may be selected. It is a core theme unifying his prior (Simon, 1947, 1951) *and* his later work (Simon, 1959, 1967, 1969, 1976, 1978a,b) that individuals are guided not by involved trade-offs but by the application of rules which are merely elaborations of the statement "engage in an action if it meets these cut-offs". Gigerenzer and Goldstein (1996) and Selten (1998) and all manner of heuristics in the cognitive psychology literature (see Gigerenzer and Selten, 1999b) effectively elaborate the exact nature of those cut-offs.

Earl (1986a,b, 1983) was one of the first to realise the broad spectrum of behaviour which becomes non-exotic and quite standard when we realise that there are ubiquitous "breaks in the chain of substitution". When there are breaks in the chain of substitution, choice becomes not a matter of involved, cognitively taxing trade-offs between various courses of action, but instead a matter of asking "does this behaviour meet situational requirements" and after eliminating those which don't, applying either some new set of cut-offs or making trade-offs as a sort of "tie-breaker".

As this would suggest, rule-triviality of preferences (definition 20) can be shown to give rise to non-substitutability, and this non-substitutability shown to preclude *outright* (without caveat) the selection of certain courses of action in the presence of others.

Theorem 9 (Rule triviality implies non-substitutability). *If preferences are rule-trivial, then any course of action a which is* not *selected by a decision rule $f_K(\cdot) \subset g(H')$, $a \notin S[f_K(\cdot)] \subset g(H')$ is nonsubstitutable for any course of action a' which is selected by that decision rule, $a' \in S[f_K(\cdot)]$. Furthermore, in the presence of such a course of action in the feasible set $a' \in B$, any action a which does not satisfy the rule $f_K(\cdot) \subset g(H')$ cannot be selected, $a \neq a^*$.*

In such a situation, choices to not engage in a particular course of action are not matters of "I'll take it eventually, but eventually hasn't eventuated", they are matters of "it just doesn't Cut It". There is no state of substitutability, and so no mix of incentives exist which would induce behavioural change. The demands of the "cut-offs" of the rule must be met first.

5.3 Fundamental non-substitutability: "I can't go without this"

A further, "deeper", more "fundamental" non-substitutability exists because of the distinction of *need* from *want* as behavioural drives. Wants are rather simple and need no particular definition to be understood; they are a visceral factor $\psi \in H$ "deep" in the psyche which constitute the basis for a conscious experience of desire. Needs, while they are similarly a visceral factor $\psi \in H$ "deep" in the psyche which constitute the basis for a conscious experience of desire, are distinct from wants.

As their etymology suggests, needs are something "necessary". A need is something we cannot, if possible, go without. They are distinct from wants insofar as wants may be "traded off" against each other. We may forgo a want ψ by some course of action and still find that course of action preferable to some other course of action which does satisfy that want on the basis that yet some *other* want ψ' outweighs it in the determination of preferences $\succeq \circ 2^{g(H')}$. The non-satiation of a need *necessarily* implies some sort of loss which cannot be regained, which is not the case with wants.

Specifically, it is necessary that needs be satisfied by a course of action in order for that course of action to be at least as preferable as any other course of action which satisfies those needs. If a course of action does not satisfy a need, it must be less preferable than a course of action which does.

Definition 25 (Needs). A need is a visceral factor ψ such that, when elicited by the environment, $\psi \in H'$, if a non-satiation relation $R_{h\psi} = \neg\psi_s$ exists in the chain of implications g_a from a course of action $a \in A'$ to the visceral factor $\psi \in H'$, its implications g_a are strictly less preferable than those $g_{a'}$ of any other course of action $a' \in 2^A$ for which there exists a satiation relation $R_{h\psi} = \psi_s$ in the chain of implications $g_{a'}$. That is, formally,

$$\exists R_{h\psi} = \neg\psi_s \in g_a \Rightarrow g_{a'} \succ g_a \ \forall a' \in 2^A : \left\{ \exists R_{h\psi} = \psi_s \in g_{a'} \right\} \quad (5.3)$$

We may now demonstrate that if a need exists, and it is possible to satiate it, no alternative which does not satisfy it will be selected.

Theorem 10 (If possible, needs can't not be met). *A course of action $a \in B$ may be selected ($a = a^*$, defined by equation 3.7) when there is some other feasible course of action $a' \in B$ for which a relation exists $\psi_s \in g(H')$ in the chain of implications $g_{a'}$ indicating the satiation of some need $\psi \in H'$ elicited by the environment only if there is no relation $\neg\psi_s \in g(H')$ in the chain of implications g_a, of that course of action a indicating the non-satiation of that need $\psi \in H'$.*

If needs exist, behaviour goes beyond the "it just doesn't cut it" type, and becomes decided by the vicissitudes of necessity: "I can't go without this". This individual can't "go without" the need being satiated, and so cannot select a course of action which would not satiate it in the presence of one which could. Unless, for instance, an individual has no particular need of survival, they *must* eat and drink for nourishment and in the ultimate cannot be induced not to do so without that behaviour being made infeasible.

Note that this consequence (theorem 10) of the definition of needs (definition 25) does not preclude their *not* being satisfied. It only forbids the individual from selecting a course of action which does not satisfy a need *if* there is another course of action which *does*.

Corollary 4 (If needs can't be met, they aren't). *A course of action $a \in B$ for which there exists a relation $\neg\psi_s \in g(H')$ in the chain of implications g_a indicating the non-satiation of a need elicited by the environment, $\psi \in H'$ may be selected, $a = a^*$, provided there is no other feasible course of action $a' \in B$ for which a relation exists $\psi_s \in g(H')$ in the chain of implications $g_{a'}$ indicating its satiation.*

An interesting and informative paradox arises out of definition 25. Observe that if we took two actions a and a' and two needs ψ and ψ' and supposed that the former action satisfied the former, but not the latter need, and the latter action satisfied the latter but not the former need, then we would find by definition 25 that $g_a \succ g_{a'}$ and $g_{a'} \succ g_a$, which is absurd. But this absurdity is important, for it indicates a potential source for decision paralysis. If those actions were more preferable than any others, $g_a, g_{a'} \succ g_{a''} \forall a'' \in B$, we would find by the "make up your mind/checkmate" theorem (theorem 3, specifically the breaking of condition 3 thereof) that this paradox would lead to the choice function being not well defined. Without more information, the individual would not be able to decide between the satiation of competing needs.

Where it does occur, this matter is not one which can be resolved by "trading off" the satiation of one need against another. Needs are, as discussed above, different to wants, they do not have obsolescence, they are either satisfied or they are not. The implication therefore is that in order to resolve this paradox we must establish as extant within personal knowledge $g(H)$ some hierarchy of needs, establishing their priority. We might define such a hierarchy thus.

Definition 26 (Hierarchy of needs). A hierarchy of needs exists if and only if there exists an index set $n \in [1, \ldots, N]$ for needs such that if some action a has implications g_a which indicate the satiation of all needs elicited $\psi \in H'$ as can be indexed by indices $n \leq \bar{n}$ below some threshold $\bar{n}$ (that is, $\exists \psi_s^n \in g_a \forall n \leq \bar{n}$), then it may be established to be strictly preferable to any other, a' for which there exists a need such as can be indexed by some index $i \leq \bar{n}$ below that same threshold $\bar{n}$ for which the implications $g_{a'}$ indicate non-satiation. That is, a hierarchy of needs exists if and only if

$$g_a \supset \psi_s^n \forall n \leq \bar{n} \Rightarrow g_a \succ g_{a'} \forall a : \exists n \leq \bar{n} \ \& \ \neg\psi_s^n \in g_{a'} \qquad (5.4)$$

Note in definition 26 that the satisfaction of any needs as can be indexed by indices above the threshold so defined is rendered moot, for such is the nature of the hierarchy that more "basic" needs in the hierarchy must be satiated before any others. Such a hierarchy as Maslow (1943, 1954) posits can then be demonstrated to potentially resolve the competition between needs for their satiation.

Theorem 11 (A hierarchy of needs may enable choice between competing needs). *If a hierarchy of needs exists, that feasible action $a \in B$ which satisfies all needs as can be indexed by an index $n \leq \bar{n}$ below some threshold $\bar{n}$, where that threshold $\bar{n}$ is the greatest threshold as can be established out* *of all feasible actions shall be selected (a = a*) if it is the only feasible action to do so.*

What this theorem demonstrates is that the hierarchy of needs can establish a priority of meeting needs. A hierarchy of wants would not necessarily conform to this result for the existence of obsolescence in wants and the ability to trade the satiation of "higher" priority wants against "lower". As Peter Earl (1983, 1986a,b) argued, a hierarchy is not a matter of trading the satiation of "higher" needs off against "lower", it is far more an element of a "constitution" in the psyche for resolving conflicts by *dictat* rather than negotiation. The hierarchy serves to establish which needs have to be met before any others can be considered[3]. This becomes important when needs are competing, for the extra information it provides in $g(H)$ may allow the individual to make a choice even in the absence of a "tie-breaker" alternative for which there is no competition between various needs for satiation.

Behaviour of this nature is contrary to substitutability as we will find without stepping outside (strictly speaking) of the spectrum of substitutability. It is not of the "I'll take it, eventually" nature. It is of the nature of "I can't go without this", and where there are multiple needs competing the conflict needs be resolved by establishing a dictatorial order in which things which "can't be gone without" will be attended to.

5.4 Complementarity: "Together or not at all"

While it is strictly speaking not of the spectrum of substitutability, complementarity is still a form of non-substitutability. Complementarity exists where two actions are "better together" than "alone".

Definition 27 (Complementarity). Actions $\alpha \subset a$ within a course of action a are complemented by those in another set α' if and only if the implications of choosing both $(g_{a \supset \alpha, \alpha'})$ are more preferable to those of choosing the former alone $(g_{a \setminus \alpha'})$, that is, if and only if

$$g_{a \supset \alpha, \alpha'} \succ g_{a \setminus \alpha'} \tag{5.5}$$

Complementarity creates the possibility that the presence of two actions in the feasible set, the possibility of their co-selection, may be the decisive factor for whether certain courses of action shall be taken or not.

Theorem 12 (Presence of complements may be decisive). *Take a preference structure $\succeq \circ 2^{g(H)}$ and a feasible set B such that some action a' has more preferable implications than all others a'' in the feasible set B, $g_{a'} \succ g_{a''}$ $\forall a'' \in B$ where that set of actions $a'' \in B$ includes some course of action* *without its complements a \ α'. If the complementarity between two sets of actions α and α' is such that they would be preferred to the originally most preferred action, $g_{a \supset \alpha, \alpha'} \succ g_{a'}$ and preferences $\succeq \circ 2^{g(H')}$ remain transitive for the preference comparison of implications of the actions a, a' and any particular other action a'' then we will find that the action containing the complements being feasible $a \in B : a \supset \alpha, \alpha'$ is sufficient for a to be selected, $a = a^*$. That is, the presence of the complementary action α' in the feasible set, $\alpha' \subset a \in B$ is sufficient for $a \supset \alpha, \alpha'$ to be selected.*

The feasibility of the action α' which complements α in a may therefore be decisive for behaviour. Once the actions α' are made feasible, their complementarity with others α induces the selection of the course of action a. Behaviour *a la* theorem 12 is of a "together or not at all" form.

5.5 If we aren't in the world of the economist, psychology matters a lot

Note in the above how broad the spectrum of behaviour is relative to that explained by the traditional neoclassical theory. *If* behaviour occurs in a context in which a state of substitutability exists, we might as well apply the theory of marginal analysis of neoclassical economics and induce behavioural change by changing incentives. However, if behaviour is not driven by "making tradeoffs" and instead is a matter of "cutoffs" or needs or complementarity, the individual is not responsive to incentives. To induce their behaviour to change requires something more fundamental; a change of capabilities (Sen, 1999) by some change of technology, a change of environment which is substantial, or a change to the structure of the psyche itself.

Notes

1. The results presented in this section are derived from a previously published paper titled "Economic Dark Matter: On the Theory of Substitutability" (see Markey-Towler, 2017a).
2. Of course, since we have not defined $\{\delta_\theta\}_{\theta=0}^{\Theta}$ to be a continuous interval in a metric space, this may be because such a point would actually lie between two points in the sequence δ_θ and $\delta_{\theta'}$, a technical problem which is irrelevant if we simply interpolate the admixture of δ_θ and $\delta_{\theta'}$ which would induce substitutability and insert it into the sequence $\{\delta_\theta\}_{\theta=0}^{\Theta}$.
3. The hierarchy of need is not sufficient to guarantee choices be made, for we might have other feasible actions which satisfy all needs as can be indexed by $n \leq \bar{n}$, breaking the final, technical, condition of theorem 11. We would require more information again to decide preference among such actions.

References

Drakopoulos, S., 1994. Hierarchical choice in economics. *Journal of Economic Surveys* 8 (2), 133–153.

Drakopoulos, S., Karayiannis, A., 2004. The historical development of hierarchical behavior in economic thought. *Journal of the History of Economic Thought* 26 (3), 363–378.

Earl, P., 1983. *The Economic Imagination*. Wheatsheaf, Brighton.

Earl, P., 1986a. A behavioural analysis of demand elasticities. *Journal of Economic Studies* 13 (3), 20–37.

Earl, P., 1986b. *Lifestyle Economics*. Harvester Wheatsheaf, Brighton.

Gigerenzer, G., Goldstein, D., 1996. Reasoning the fast and frugal way: Models of bounded rationality. *Psychological Review* 103 (4), 650–669.

Gigerenzer, G., Selten, R. (Eds.), 1999b. *Bounded Rationality*. Dahlem Workshop Reports. MIT Press, Cambridge, MA.

Markey-Towler, B., 2017a. *Economic Dark Matter: On the Theory of Substitutability*, available at SSRN: https://papers.ssrn.com/sol3/papers.cfm?abstract_id=2971744

Marshall, A., 1890. *Principles of Economics*, 8th Edition. Macmillan, London.

Maslow, A., 1943. A theory of human motivation. *Psychological Review* 50 (4), 370–396.

Maslow, A., 1954. *Motivation and Personality*. Harper & Brothers, New York.

Selten, R., 1998. Aspiration adaptation theory. *Journal of Mathematical Psychology* 42, 191–214.

Sen, A., 1999. *Commodities and Capabilities*. Oxford University Press, Oxford.

Simon, H., 1947. *Administrative Behavior*, 4th Edition. The Free Press, New York.

Simon, H., 1951. A formal theory of the employment relationship. *Econometrica* 19 (3), 293–305.

Simon, H., 1955. A behavioural model of rational choice. *Quarterly Journal of Economics* 69 (1), 99–118.

Simon, H., 1959. Theories of decision-making in economics and behavioural science. *American Economic Review* 49 (3), 3.

Simon, H., 1967. Motivation and emotional controls of cognition. *Psychological Review* 74 (1), 29–39.

Simon, H., 1969. *The Sciences of the Artificial*. MIT Press, Cambridge, MA.

Simon, H., 1976. *Method and Appraisal in Economics*. Cambridge University Press, Cambridge, Ch. From substantive to procedural rationality, pp. 129–148.

Simon, H., 1978a. On how to decide what to do. *Bell Journal of Economics* 9 (2), 494–507.

Simon, H., 1978b. Rationality as a process and as product of thought. *American Economic Review* 68 (2), 1–16.

6 Properties of the psyche and their influence on behaviour
Explanations and predictions

We finally turn to consider how the theory we have proposed contains explanations and predictions of a number of psychological and behavioural phenomena observed by psychologists, neuroscientists, sociologists and economists. A particular contribution of this work is to demonstrate how hitherto seemingly particular and disconnected psychological and behavioural phenomena are actually aspects of particular stages of the same decision-making process, aspects we would *expect* to observe in human thought and behaviour.

These phenomena coexist within a unified, and relatively tractable formalism, something theories (such as Thaler, 1980, and Kahneman and Tversky, 1979) seeking to modify the standard economic model of choice to account for this or that set of deviations from its predictions have struggled to do to any great extent. Instead of being pathological "biases" as they are commonly referred to in the behavioral economics literature (Mehta, 2013) (misspelt deliberately after the American fashion) to be accounted for by "Portable Extensions of Existing Models" (Rabin, 2013a,b), these phenomena are revealed to be nothing less than natural – indeed reasonable – aspects of individuals' psychology.

We will begin by establishing that behaviour can be changed by changing the environment in which it takes place without constraint. We will then consider the exactitudes of the psychological process by which this might be facilitated, first as regards the form of the perception mapping, then, taking this in hand, as regards the interaction of the form of analysis with preference and behaviour. We shall conclude by considering some issues in the evolution of the mind, the structure in which the psychological process takes place.

6.1 Context contingency of behaviour

In our theory, it is possible for behaviour to change between two courses of action without altering the set of feasible actions. In the words of Thaler and Sunstein (2008), it is possible for individuals to be "nudged". This is actually rather obvious in the present theory, for by changing the environment an individual faces, and by thus changing what they are thinking at a conscious or subconscious level, we are changing the way they think about how to behave.

Theorem 13 (Behaviour may be context-contingent). *Take two environments v_N and v'_N such that two courses of action are feasible in both situations, $a^*, a' \in B \subset A'(v_N)$ and $a^*, a' \in B' \subset A'\left(v'_N\right)$ (where $A'(v_N)$ and $A'\left(v'_N\right)$ are defined according to definition 9), and suppose the individual decides in the initial environment to choose some course of action $a^* = \{a \in B : g_a \succ g_{a''} \; \forall \; a'' \in B\}$. We will find the other course of action selected, $a' = \{a \in B' : g'_{a'} \succ g'_{a''} \; \forall a'' \in B'\}$, and a change of behaviour $a^* \to a'$ if and only if the change in environment $v_N \to v'_N$ is sufficient to induce an understanding in which the implications of a' can be established to be strictly preferred to the implications of any other alternative. That is,*

$$g\left(\rho\left(v'_N\right)\backslash\{R_{hh'}\}\right) : g'_{a'} \succ g'_{a''} \; \forall \, a'' \in B' \tag{6.1}$$

where $g'_a, g'_{a'} \subset g\left(\rho\left(v'_N\right)\backslash\{R_{hh'}\}\right)$

Preferences in the sense of economic theory over feasible courses of action then are contingent, not given. They are dependent in theory as in reality (Kahneman and Tversky, 1979; Tversky and Kahneman, 1981; Kahneman, 2003; Rabin, 1998) on the context in which those courses of action are perceived, the perception of the environment in which the individual finds themselves and the way they think about it.

This shows us something interesting beyond being able to capture the reversal of preferences. The standard tool for implementing, especially, economic policies has hitherto been manipulating the prices of a good or service, which is predicated on the argument of Becker (1962) that prices are the key determinants of economic behaviour in the aggregate by making behaviour feasible or infeasible. This theorem tells us instead that one need not resort to such drastic measures. This is important because it is very difficult to make a behaviour totally infeasible at any level and merely making it feasible is not sufficient for it to be engaged in. Instead our theory allows for what Thaler and Sunstein (2008) have called "nudges", structuring the choice environment so that thinking about behaviour is altered, either by changing the "choice architecture", i.e. the context in which alternatives are presented, or by doing so in a more old-fashioned manner by engaging in public reasoning about the consequences and desirability of a particular action.

Our theory does however show us also that there is a complexity in changing behaviour by manipulating context. It is not enough to simply alter the preferability between the implications associated with a particular action a^* currently selected, and another alternative a' that is to be selected, because when the choice environment changes so do in principle the outcomes expected of *all* alternatives. Hence in order for there to be a change of behaviour, the implications of the new behaviour must not merely be able to be established preferred to the implications of the old, the implications must be preferred to any *other* alternative which becomes available. We might warn people about the dangers of not investing sufficient money for retirement and make it preferable to using that money for consumption, but we must also make investing money more preferable than any other alternative, such as, say, simply leaving that money in a low-yield savings deposit.

Context contingency and the multiple self: a theory of "willpower"

When we interpret $g(H)$ as the system of all personal constructs in the style of Kelly (1963), and $g(H')$ as their application to form understanding of percepts $H' \subset \rho\,(v_N)$ of particular environments v_N, then we notice that contained in theorem 13 is a theory of how the "multiple selves" of any individual can affect their behaviour.

Discussed at length in Elster (1986) is the concept that we have not one uniform system of beliefs and thought processes within $g(H)$, but various subsystems $\{g_\lambda\}_{\lambda \in \Lambda} \subset g(H)$ of personal constructs associated with different "selves" Λ. The shift of thinking $g(\rho\,(v_N)\backslash\{R_{hh'}\}) \to g(\rho\,(v'_N)\backslash\{R'_{hh'}\})$ induced by a change of environment $v_N \to v'_N$ might involve a shift between different selves λ and λ' and their thought, $g_\lambda \approx g(\rho\,(v_N)\,\backslash\{R_{hh'}\})$ and $g_{\lambda'} \approx g(\rho\,(v'_N)\backslash\{R'_{hh'}\})$, evoked within the process of thinking $g(H') \subset g(H)$. If such a change satisfies theorem 13, it is possible that this generates a change of behaviour. The classic example is the phenomenon of *akrasia*, literally "lacking command" when the consequentialist, rational, fastidious self λ is elicited in one environment v_N and the hedonistic, emotion-dominated and myopic self λ' is elicited when the environment changes $v_N \to v'_N$ (Ainslie, 1986; Rorty, 1986) – the shift often thought to underlie risky but pleasurable behaviours. The emotional, socially conscious self λ'' may support *akrasic* "herd-following" behaviour (Baddeley, 2010, 2013, 2015), against the personal judgments less prominent in, say, the thinking $g_{\lambda''} \approx g\left(\rho\left(v'_N\right) \backslash \{R_{hh'}\}\right)$ than in the thinking $g_\lambda \approx g(\rho\ (v_N) \backslash \{R_{hh'}\})$ in the fear of being "left out" by not conforming to other individuals' actions.

This furnishes the beginnings of a coherent theory of "willpower" fairly consonant with the findings of Roy Bauermeister (see Tierney and Bauermeister, 2011) when coupled with the concept of entropic decay in understanding $g(H)$ of the world. If at some point the inner or outer environment calls forth the myopic self, one may succumb to *akrasia*. But the more the "rational", "controlled" self is elicited it becomes strengthened, and the less the myopic self is called forth it decays. As we discuss now the concepts of salience (specifically the hold of visceral factors on attention), we may also discover an explanation (rising stress levels) for why it becomes more likely willpower will fail to rule the more an individual acts in the world.

6.2 Salience in perception

It is perhaps the oldest known phenomena in psychology that we do not necessarily perceive all that is presented to us (Vernon, 1962). Our perception is context-dependent.

Definition 28 (Context-contingence of perception). Perception $\rho\ (\cdot)$ is context contingent if for a particular environment v_N, perception $\rho\ (v' \subset v_N)$ of information $v' \subset v_N$ contained within that environment as defined by 6 is not the same as perception of that information on its own $\rho\ (v')$. That is, context-contingency of perception exists if

$$\rho(v') \neq \rho(v' \subset v_N) \tag{6.2}$$

This is a bit of a challenging definition on the face of it, for rarely will we be able to envisage a scenario where the information v' can be perceived in isolation from a context, so that $v_N = v'$. However, this is not in fact necessary in order to determine that context-contingency exists according to definition 28.

Theorem 14 (Testing for context-contingency of perception). *Perception* $\rho\ (\cdot)$ *is context-contingent according to definition 28 if we can find two particular environments* v_N *and* v'_N *such that* $v' \subset v_N$ *and* $v' \subset v'_N$ *and that*

$$\rho\left(v' \subset v_N\right) \neq \rho\left(v' \subset v'_N\right) \tag{6.3}$$

This is a useful enough conception of the notion of context-contingency of perception, but we can also theorise why such a sensitivity arises. It is well known (Vernon, 1962) that the most important fact about perception is that it can be characterised by an unusually instructive tautology: we notice only what is noticeable. We notice what makes a greater "impression" on our sensory organs and our nervous system. We only notice and perceive certain information if it "stands out", if it is "salient".

Theorem 15 (Salience leads to context-contingency of perception). *Suppose any subset $v' \subset v_N$ of information contained within an environment v_N and that environment itself may be mapped to a metric $\sigma : 2^{V_N} \rightarrow \mathbb{R}$ representing the overall "noticeability" of that information with respect to the senses. Suppose further that percepts may be perceived if and only if the information corresponding to them is sufficiently salient relative to the environment*

$$h \in \rho\left(v' \subset v_N\right) \Leftrightarrow \sigma\left(v'\right) - \sigma\left(v_N\right) \geq \bar{\sigma} \tag{6.4}$$

for some individual-specific constant $\bar{\sigma} \geq 0$ we call the perception threshold and some information v' we select such that $h \in H$ is its percept $(v' : h = \rho\left(v'\right))$. If V_N is sufficiently large that there exists a particular environment v_N with a larger noticeability than v' adjusted for the perception threshold $\bar{\sigma}$, $(\exists v_N \subset V_N : \sigma\left(v_N\right) > \sigma\left(v'\right) - \bar{\sigma})$ then perception $\rho\left(\cdot\right)$ is context-contingent.

We might generalise this theorem so that σ maps to $\mathbb{R}^5$, metrics of the five senses of sight, smell, sound, touch and taste (though sight can have at least three further metrics of depth, breadth and height), or see σ as a composite reflecting salience with respect to some admixture of all five. In any case, a salience property such as 6.4 in perception $\rho\left(\cdot\right)$ is sufficient for it to be sensitive to salient information and thus contingent on the particular environment v_N in which information $v' \subset v_N$ is presented.

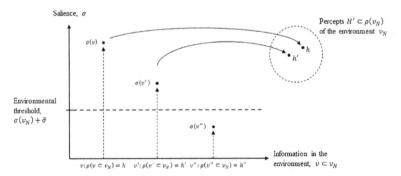

Figure 6.1 The salience property: if information has sufficient salience, "noticeability", impression on the sensory organs, then the percept corresponding to it will be perceived.

It is easy to understate the importance of this result. What it means is that what the individual *sees*, their very vision, can be changed not only by changing the basic content of the environment, but by simply changing the presentation of that content. The way we structure a decision environment can change even what a person actually sees.

The implications of theorem 15 allow us to reduce a number of phenomena in psychology and behaviour back to the phenomenon of salience: the tendency to account for "extreme" events, the dominance of visceral factors (emotions) in the decision process, and the discounting of the future at sharply increasing rates.

Extreme events in perception: more likely to be accounted for

An extreme event is, by definition, extreme, out of the ordinary, something which "stands out". An ordinary event, by definition, is the opposite. It is ordinary, something which does *not* "stand out". The tendency to perceive extreme events and attribute them a significance in decision making far exceeding their relative frequency (Tversky and Kahneman, 1974; Kahneman and Tversky, 1979; Taleb, 2007) is really a rather quotidian matter in the present theory. Extreme events are salient, they are more noticeable than ordinary events which are, by virtue of their ordinariness, less noticeable. They are therefore more likely than ordinary events to satisfy the salience property (equation 6.4) in any given environment, and be accounted for in the individual's thinking. In the present time, we do not notice the thousands of safe airplane flights made everyday for this is ordinary, commonplace. It doesn't factor into our thoughts and behaviour nearly as much as the extreme events of 2014 when not one but two Malaysian Air planes were lost (one disappearing but for some scraps of metal, the other shot down over a war zone) and every single person on them killed. The latter is unusual, extreme, and is noticeable and thus more likely to be accounted for in our decision making.

The passions and the fury: the hold of the visceral factors on the psyche

Visceral factors in decision making, the emotions and what used to be called the "passions" in an older English are again something which almost by definition "stand out" and *command* the attention of the individual (Loewenstein, 1996, 2000; Elster, 1998). The salience property (equation 6.4) explains to us why they hold a significance in decision making which is commensurate with their impact on the sensory organs. If we imagine a spectrum of impressions upon the sensory system along which we array the objects and

Figure 6.2 Salience in perception: the vibrant patterns and textures of this tree readily announce themselves to the senses and are noticed – the little bird in the branches, not so much.

events in the world, the visceral factors of the psyche, the passions and the fury, lie well toward the stronger end, and in fact some might argue that they define its endpoint. They are more likely than any other object or event to be perceived in any given environment and play a role in the decision making process. They are therefore a significant factor in the "multiple selves" theory mentioned previously and the theory of willpower. We are likely to observe such impulsive selves elicited when stress levels are raised, for instance after a prolonged period of activity, and the emotional self is rising into thought because emotions are salient enough for that to occur.

Marketers have practiced the exploitation of this phenomenon since the Mad Men (Madison Avenue marketers) discovered Freudian psychology in the 1950s (Packard, 1957), but of course politicians and professional manipulators have known this since antiquity. Aristotle in the *Rhetoric*, learning the lessons of Thucydides in particular about the conduct of public debate in the Athenian *demos* during the Peloponnesian war, and those lessons Plato and Xenophon didn't quite see in the case of Socrates, knew this better than most and so ascribed especial importance to the appeal of the rhetorician to *pathos*, to *emotion*, rather than *logos*, reason. *Pathos* commands our attention because it is visceral and noticeable, *logos* of course may too, but not in the same manner as a matter of course.

The role of time in perception: disregarding the future

Perhaps unorthodox at first glance, though rather intuitive at a second, the salience property 6.4 provides us with an explanation of the widely observed phenomenon of discounting the future, commonly called "hyperbolic discounting". The present formalism goes beyond the relatively crude discounting exercise of behavioural economics (see Frederick et al., 2002) in which a discount factor is multiplied by some quantification of future consequences of present actions to suggest psychological processes underlying behaviour consistent with such discounting. There may indeed be conscious discounting, disregard, for future consequences of present actions in the construed relations $\{R_{hh'}\}$ between an act a and future consequences thereof. But a more intriguing possibility is that at a more fundamental level, in addition to this, the future is simply less salient than the present.

We feel what we are feeling now. We feel what we *will* feel only at a remove – as what we *will* feel. The contents of the future are not available to us, but as they are construed by us to exist in the future, they are ultimately a matter of anticipation within expectations (construed by relations $R_{hh'}$) between percepts of internal information in v_N in the individual's understanding of the world-system $g(H)$. They are less salient compared with the experience of the here and now, rapidly less so the further into the future they are, and thus increasingly likely to "fail" the salience property (equation 6.4), not be perceived, and not be accounted for in the individual's understanding of their environment $g(H')$.[1] This helps us to understand why sometimes we *do* account as fully as we could for the future, and why other times we do *not*. In the

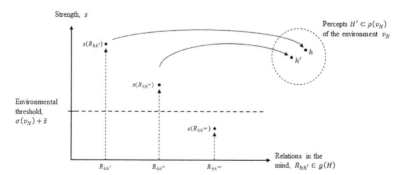

Figure 6.3 The "follow-on" property: if a certain percept h is connected by a relation $R_{hh'}$ of sufficient to another, h' the perception of the former, $\rho\ (v_N)$ $\supset h$ will cause the perception of the latter, h'.

standard models of "hyperbolic discounting", the same "discount factor" is applied to quantified future consequences irrespective of the magnitude it is applied to. Here we may find that the more significant, the more extreme, the more salient the future consequences of actions in the present, whether positive or negative, the more likely they are to be accounted for in the present.

Consider, for instance, contemporary controversies on climate change. Some "alarmists" expect it will cause the collapse of life support systems on earth, rather salient. "Denialists" reject such expectations, and instead tend to expect significant commercial costs in the present of changing emissions. The one finds it more challenging to believe their behaviour must change in the present (the denialist), while the other (the alarmist), looking to what they believe to be the future, does not.

6.3   Chains in perception

David Hume (1777, p.14) noted that our thoughts "introduce one another with a certain degree of method and regularity". Often they "follow" one another in a sequence. Of course we know that this is commensurate with brain function – the electrical impulses which support thought travel progressively through synaptic networks (Kandel et al., 2013; Sapolsky, 2017). It would therefore appear there is a reflexivity in the form of the perception mapping such that it depends on the structure of the mind $g(H)$. This gives rise to what we might call the "follow-on" property of perception.

Definition 29 ("Follow-on" property of perception). Supposing that the metric $s : R \to \mathbb{R}_+$ mapping relations to their "strength" is commensurable with the "salience" metric $\sigma : 2^{V_N} \to \mathbb{R}$, if a percept h is connected to another h' by a sufficiently strong connection $R_{hh'} : s(R_{hh'}) - \sigma(v_N) \geq \bar{s}$ in the mind, then the perception $h \in \rho\,(v_N)$ of the former percept will cause the perception of the latter, $h' \in \rho\,(v_N)$. That is, for some individual specific threshold $\bar{s}$

$$h \in H' \,\&\, \exists R_{hh'} \in g(H) : s(R_{hh'}) - \sigma(v_N) \geq \bar{s} \Rightarrow h' \in H' \qquad (6.5)$$

This commensurability is not entirely unreasonable to assume, for both s and σ are feelings of "intensity", and it reduces the number of our parameters.[2]

An important (though formally more complex) generalisation of the follow-on property allows for *groups* of percepts, sets $\{h_n\}_{n \in N} \subset H'$, to cause the perception, $h' \in H'$ of some other, h', if the *combined* strength of their connections to it, the set $\{R_{h_n}h'\}_{n \in N}$, is sufficiently large.[3] That perception may be contingent on mental networks in this further manner allows for categorisations of higher-order abstraction to emerge in perception of the form "attributes *a*, *b* and *c* suggest *d*", which are important for cognition and language.

Now by extrapolating the follow-on property, we may demonstrate an interesting result.

Theorem 16 (Percepts elicited by chains of thought). *Suppose there exists a chain of thought $g = \left\{ R_{hh'} \in g(H) : hh' \in \left\{ h_k h_{k+1} \right\}_{k=0}^{K} \subset g(H) \right\}$ such that every relation $R_{hh'} \in g$ is sufficiently strong for the follow-on property of perception to hold. If $h_0 \in \rho\ (v_{N(g)})$, then the chain of thought g is elicited in analysis $g(H')$, $g \subset g(H')$. That is*

$$h_0 \in \rho\left(v_{N(g)}\right) \ \& \ s(R_{hh'}) - \sigma\left(v_{N(g)}\right) \geq \bar{s} \, \forall R_{hh'} \in g \Rightarrow g \subset g(H') \ \ (6.6)$$

Perception is thus contingent on *personality*, the way in which we "construe events" (Kelly, 1963). What we *see* depends on "who we are" in a sense, and so we can make inferences about events even without the events existing in the external environment. In a sense, we may "call up" memories of the past, or imagine, construe, connections between events which have not yet been observed.

The power of implication and suggestion

That whole chains of thought might be called into existence by perception because of their connection to certain objects and events in the environment means that particular ways of structuring the environment may suggest or imply particular views of it to the individual. Optical illusions play on such suggestion and implication. By placing certain objects in the field of vision we might suggest or imply a particular perception to the individual, knowing (perhaps only subconsciously ourselves) how our perception is guided by the manner in which we construe events.

Suggestion and implication are important in the context of interpersonal relationships too. The Socrates of both Plato and Xenophon said exactly the wrong thing in his *Apologia* when defending himself against the charges of corrupting the youth, failing to honour the Athenian gods and introducing new ones. Not many years later Aristotle would remark in the *Rhetoric* that the speaker must be cautious to not inflame passions contrary to the behaviour the speaker wishes, realising the power of implication and suggestion. Socrates argued to varying success against the three charges laid against him, but he went further to assert his wisdom and integrity over his

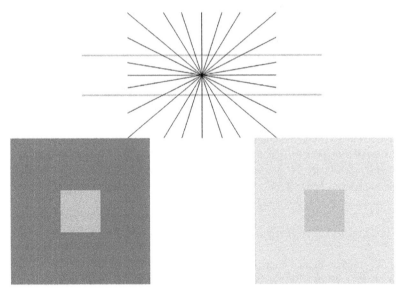

Figure 6.4 Suggestion and implication in optical illusion: the lines radiating from the centre suggest circularity and imply curvature of the straight parallel lines, while the shades of the outer boxes relative to the inner boxes suggest the inner box that is darker than its surrounds is darker than the other inner box, when they are actually the same.

compatriots, specifically indicting them for their vicious lack of integrity in the recent and spectacularly disastrous Peloponnesian War compared to his own good conduct. From what we know from Thucydides of the vengeful fickleness and pride of the Athenian personality, this was not a particularly wise move if Socrates was not (as might be argued) world-weary and wanting to die. Socrates would hardly have been suggesting equanimitous associations to the minds of his jurors, and of course we know the famous outcome that when offered (as was customary) the right to propose his own punishment and using it to recommend he be honoured by the city rather than punished, Socrates was sentenced to death by a greater majority than had found him guilty.

The representativeness and availability heuristics

Personality contingent perception reduces what has been called the "representativeness heuristic" and "availability heuristic" (Tversky and Kahneman, 1974, 1981; Rabin, 1998; Kahneman, 2003) to a property of the psyche. With respect to the former, we tend to find that we use one situation

Figure 6.5 If the height of the middle building is taken as representative we would think the heights of these buildings quite different. They're actually within 20 meters of each other's height.

Figure 6.6 Churches? Certainly a concept more "available" to our mind when considering buildings which look like this. Actually the one on the left is a function hall, and on the right, a nightclub.

and our understanding thereof to form our understanding of some other, we judge it to be "representative" of another. Here, we would find the one object or event, h_1 adjudged to be representative of another, h_0 in the connection $R_{h_0 h_1}$ and so the thoughts attendant upon h_1 become applied to the other h_0 by theorem 16 by their being construed to be following from a representative object or event. In the latter heuristic, we apply information which is readily "available" to the mind for characterising some object or event. The elements h' are readily "available" to be related to h_0 by virtue of their being connected sufficiently strongly by certain connections $R_{h_0 h'}$.

Clarity in high-stress environments

Notice finally the caveat on the follow-on property of the threshold of "sufficient" strength, $s(R_{hh'}) \geq \bar{s} + \sigma(v_N)$. What happens if we observe a "Red Queen" effect here, say in a "high stress" environment, when $\sigma(v_N)$ is quite high as a great deal of impression is being made on the sensory organs and nervous system by the environment? In such an environment, the follow-on property and theorem 16 which follows from it would dictate that only very strong relations will satisfy the follow on property. This might lead to the phenomenon of "focus" (as the saying goes: "nothing concentrates the mind like the fear of being hanged") or "going to pieces" in the face of "adversity". Comparatively few connections would be able to satisfy the follow-on property of perception to support thought in a high-stress environment. What would distinguish the former from the latter case would be the individual's ability to satisfy the conditions of the "make up your mind/checkmate" theorem (theorem 3) on the basis of a comparatively small set of considerations, giving the appearance of "calm dispatch" in the manner spoken of by Herbert Simon (1947) in the context of "expertise".

6.4   Anchoring in analysis

It is commonly observed, well known in fact for at least one hundred years (Veblen, 1899), that alternative courses of action $a \in 2^A$ or descriptors of reality $\delta \in \Delta \subset H$ do not influence what we think, $g(H') \subset g(H)$, as absolutes but rather as *relative* to some other thing. Kelly (1963) and Hinkle (1965) emphasise that objects can make no sense except by reference to some other thing, what they call "axes" for characterising objects in perception. Where outcomes of behaviour and objects and events must be adjudged relative to some characterisation, we will say that thinking requires "anchors".

   In the present formalism, anchors are descriptors $\bar{\delta} \in \Delta \subset H$ of objects and events in the world, and any relativity is reflected in relations $R_{h\bar{\delta}} \in g(H)$ or $R_{\bar{\delta}h}$ between percepts $h \in H$ of the objects of reality and those anchors. Any further relations $R_{hh'} \in g(H)$ of the percept of the object of

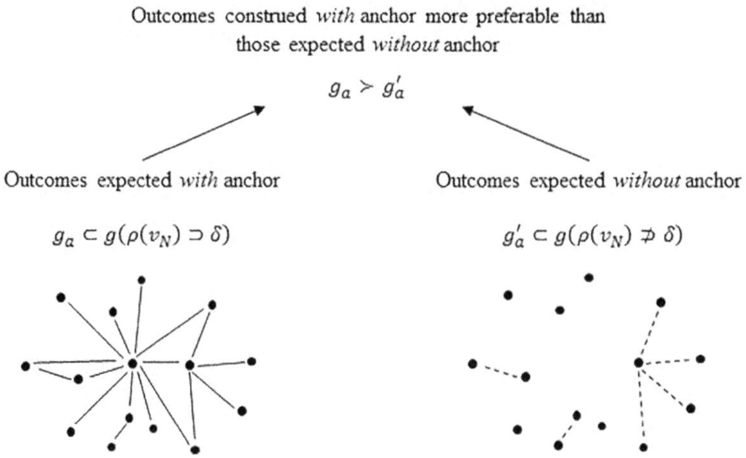

Outcomes construed *with* anchor more preferable than
those expected *without* anchor

$$g_a \succ g'_a$$

Outcomes expected *with* anchor

$$g_a \subset g(\rho(v_N) \supset \delta)$$

Outcomes expected *without* anchor

$$g'_a \subset g(\rho(v_N) \not\supset \delta)$$

Figure 6.7 Non-inert anchors may not only change the structure of thinking, but the form of thoughts which might be contingent upon them.

reality h may be then conditioned upon this relativity with respect to the anchor $\bar{\delta}$, for instance $\{R_{hh'} \in g(H)\} = \{\cdot | R_{h\bar{\delta}} \in g(H)\}$. Anchors will be primarily of interest to us if they are *non-inert*, if they change thinking about a situation enough to have an effect on the aesthetical feeling about the outcomes an individual expects to follow various courses of action g_a.

Definition 30 (Non-inert anchors). Suppose that we have two environments v_N and v'_N such that an anchor $\bar{\delta}$ is present in one but not the other, that is, $\rho(v_N)\backslash\{R_{hh'}\} = H' \not\supset \bar{\delta}$ and $\rho(v'_N)\backslash\{R'_{hh'}\} = H' \cup \bar{\delta}$. The anchor $\bar{\delta}$ is *non-inert* if and only if, when it is elicited by the environment in perception, $\bar{\delta} \in \rho(v_N)$, the implications $g_a \subset g(\rho(v_N) \supset \bar{\delta})$ of some act a contained within thinking about the environment $g(\rho(v_N) \supset \bar{\delta})$ change sufficiently to make those implications more preferable than the implications would have been were that anchor not elicited by the environment in perception $\bar{\delta} \notin \rho(v_N)$. That is, an anchor $\bar{\delta}$ is non-inert if and only if

$$g_a \subset g(\rho(v_N) \supset \bar{\delta}) \succ g'_a \subset g(\rho(v'_N) \not\supset \bar{\delta}) \tag{6.7}$$

The role of these anchors in the psyche and behaviour is illustrated in the following result, which demonstrates that the presence of psychological anchors may be decisive in causing behavioural changes.

Theorem 17 (Psychological anchors may change behaviour). *Suppose that we have two actions a and a' and two environments v_N and v'_N such that an anchor is present in one but not the other, that is, $\rho(v_N)\backslash\{R_{hh'}\} = H' \not\supset \bar{\delta}$ and $\rho(v'_N)\backslash\{R'_{hh'}\} = H' \cup \bar{\delta}$. Suppose further that a and a' remain feasible and that all implications $g_{a''}$ of other actions $a'' \in B$ remain preference-comparable but non-preferable to the implications of those actions g_a and $g_{a'}$. If this anchor is sufficiently non-inert that it reverses the preferability between the two courses of action, that is, $g_{a'} \succ g_a$ when $g_a, g_{a'} \subset g\left(\rho\left(v_N\right)\backslash\{R_{hh'}\}\right)$ and $g_a \succ g_{a'}$ when $g_a, g_{a'} \subset g\left(\rho\left(v'_N\right)\backslash\{R'_{hh'}\}\right)$, then the change in environment $v_N \rightarrow v'_N$ which causes the anchor $\bar{\delta}$ to be introduced into perception, $\bar{\delta} \in \rho(v'_N)$ causes a change of behaviour $a' \rightarrow a$. That is, the change in environment $v_N \rightarrow v'_N$ causes it to be the case that*

$$\rho(v_N) \not\supset \bar{\delta} \rightarrow \rho(v'_N) \supset \bar{\delta} \Rightarrow a' = a^* \rightarrow a = a^* \tag{6.8}$$

Anchors change the way we think about any particular environment. They may change them wholesale even if thought structures are particularly contingent on them. If they change thinking enough, they may even be sufficient to change the way we act in the world, even if they seem irrational. Dan Ariely (2008) gives the example of an experiment which showed that including an option nobody actually wanted (a print subscription alone for the same price as a print *and* electronic subscription) acted as an anchor in decisions to subscribe to the *Economist* magazine to change the choices people made, because it made the option it was "closer to" (a print *and* electronic subscription) seem more preferable. In another example,[4] Ariely hypothesised whether the option of having your car stolen would influence one's choice between a holiday in Paris and a holiday in Rome. If that were to serve as an anchor which causes one to begin thinking about terrorist incidents involving cars in France, or theft in the streets of Rome, that anchor might indeed and fairly reasonably cause your whole thinking to change, and your behaviour with it.

Any object or event in the environment which changes thinking significantly is an anchor, and as Kelly (1963) and Hinkle (1965) argued, as "axes" for classifying objects and events they are *necessary* for thinking. Thus the phenomenon of anchoring in personal constructs has an extraordinary universality (Earl, 2015). Emotions, needs and wants serve to anchor thinking when they are elicited by the environment by changing the whole manner of thinking about various courses of action. Symbols which crystallise and condense whole systems of thought in the style of Jungian Archetypes are powerful anchors for thought. Even quotidian categories "A is not-A" are vital anchors for guiding the whole structure of our thinking about our environment (Hayek, 1952). As long as, when

Figure 6.8 The effect of a non-inert anchor: consider the photograph on the left, how comfortable would you be walking into this building in casual clothes? Suppose you took a step back and saw the sign in the photograph on the right, how would you feel doing that now?

elicited in perception, a particular object or event has a significant effect on one's thinking about a situation, it may be a sufficient anchor of thought even to change behaviour.

Prospect theory as an elaboration of the effect of non-inert anchors

The concept of anchoring subsumes and extends three of the four phenomena incorporated within Kahneman and Tversky's "prospect theory" (Kahneman and Tversky, 1979). The first, probability weighting, is already incorporated into psychological theory by the salience property described previously, but theorem 17 goes further than prospect theory with respect to the other three by explicitly and formally connecting them to the behaviour they support where prospect theory merely links them to a particular form of a "utility function" (Kahneman and Tversky, 1979; Barberis, 2013).

A great deal of decision-making is "reference-dependent", which is to say that decisions are not based on a consideration of absolutes, but rather actions or outcomes *relative* to some reference level. We know, for instance, that it is not the satisfaction brought by consumption alone that drives behaviour, but rather consumption *relative* to the consumption of some reference group in the famous display of "conspicuous consumption" (Veblen, 1898; Duesenberry, 1949; Galbraith, 1958; Hirsch, 1977; Frank, 2011). We also know that a large part of our life satisfaction is derived from our income *relative* to our neighbours' or our own past income (Easterlin, 2001; Layard, 2011; Clark et al., 2008). In the words of H. L. Mencken:

"Wealth – any income that is at least one hundred dollars more a year than the income of one's wife's sister's husband".

Reference levels are anchors $\bar{\delta}$ which take the form of social comparatives or personal comparatives in the past or aspirational futures. If they are related to some action or outcome relevant to it by some anchoring relation $R_{h\bar{\delta}}$, they cause some action to become more preferable than it otherwise would. The presence of this reference-level in perception then may, by theorem 17, cause a change of behaviour relative to what would otherwise be the case. This narrative holds for whatever anchor, course of action, or set of outcomes we should care to define.

If we find the relation $R_{h\bar{\delta}}$ to indicate some form of "loss", we tend to find that it has a greater negative impact on the preferability of outcomes expected to follow from it $\{R_{hh'} \in g(H)\} = \{\cdot|R_{h\bar{\delta}} \in g(H)\}$ than positive impact were it to indicate some form of "gain". The "good" consequences of gaining Something (for many of us) always seem to be less potent than the "bad" consequences of "losing" that Something. Kahneman and Tversky (1979) account for "loss aversion" by supposing that the "utility" function is kinked and has a more steeply negative slope in losses than positive slope in gains. In the present formalism, the presence of some anchor which would create the possibility of losses would, by loss aversion, make the implications of any action which avoided losses more preferable. This, in turn, by theorem 17 could cause a change of behaviour when the anchor is present in perception relative to when it is not. This explains two further phenomena: the "endowment effect", whereby something has a greater value once you deem yourself to be in possession of it and might "lose" it, and the "preference for default options", when the *status quo* becomes something one may lose.

Similarly, if the relation $R_{h\bar{\delta}}$ were to indicate some form of loss or gain, we tend to find a change of attitude to the riskiness of the outcomes to be obtained in the relations $\{R_{hh'} \in g(H)\} = \{\cdot|R_{h\bar{\delta}} \in g(H)\}$ which follow from it – what is known as the "Reflection effect, attitudes to risk". Specifically, losses tend to be associated with positive attitudes to risk, while gains tend to be associated with positive attitudes to lesser risk. Kahneman and Tversky (1979) account for this by supposing the "utility" function switches from convexity to concavity as we move from losses to gains. Our present formalism is more direct. If some action may entail possible losses, it becomes more preferable in its implications the riskier they are. If some action may entail possible gains, it becomes more preferable in its implications the less risky they are. By theorem 17, the presence of the anchor in perception when changing attitudes to risk exist may cause behaviour to be otherwise than it would have been. The presence of loss aversion and changing attitudes to risk mean that we become more willing to gamble when faced with a loss, or are trying to "recoup" one.

6.5 Experienced vs. expected relations in analysis

It has often been observed in common sense, and also behavioural economics, that there is a difference between expectation and experience (Kahneman and Thaler, 2006). In the present theory this is rather *de rigeur*. We would expect for a differential to appear between the relations construed prior to and realised after an experience, for the environment changes. After an individual decides to act, the environment changes $v_N \rightarrow v'_N$ naturally due to the progression of time, the individual's perceptions are likely to change $\rho(v_N) \rightarrow \rho(v'_N)$, and the set of construed relations between the objects of reality will change with them $g(\rho(v_N) \backslash \{R_{hh'}\}) \rightarrow g(\rho(v'_N) \backslash \{R_{hh'}\}')$. The consequences which follow any particular act, construed or perceived to be experienced, g_a are also similarly likely to change, so

$$g_a \subset g(\rho(v_N) \backslash \{R_{hh'}\}) \rightarrow g'_a \subset g(\rho(v'_N) \backslash \{R_{hh'}\}') \tag{6.9}$$

and

$$g_a \subset g(\rho(v_N) \backslash \{R_{hh'}\}) \neq g'_a \subset g(\rho(v'_N) \backslash \{R_{hh'}\}') \tag{6.10}$$

on this basis. The first set of implications, consequences, $g_a \subset g(\rho(v_N) \backslash \{R_{hh'}\})$ are construed, the second set, $g'_a \subset g(\rho(v'_N) \backslash \{R_{hh'}\}')$ are experienced if $a = a^*$ (the selected alternative), and construed still if $a \neq a^*$.

Apart from the fairly trifling likelihood that the environment itself changes, there are psychological reasons this differential may appear. The expectations $g_a \subset g(\rho(v_N) \backslash \{R_{hh'}\})$ prior to the realisation of behaviour are formed between *salient* information, which is not the same as salient information after the fact. So our perception of the environment may change as a result of information becoming more salient to us.

The salience property may serve to open a differential between expectations $g(\rho(v_N) \backslash \{R_{hh'}\})$ and experience $g(\rho(v'_N) \backslash \{R_{hh'}\}')$ due to the durative nature of experience. Experience occurs over a duration (Bergson, 1946) and displays "peaks" and "troughs" and "plateaus" of sensory experience. The "peaks" of experience are so called because they have a greater impact on our sensory organs. We can say that they are more salient, more noticeable, almost by definition, and more likely therefore to satisfy the salience property (equation 6.4) and be accounted for in our understanding of the environment. Hence the "peaks" of experience are more likely to be dominant in our experience than any other part of that experience. The agony of the marathon runner toward the beginning of the end of the 42.195 kilometers is far more likely to satisfy the salience property and drive their understanding of the experience than the "dull roar" present when they "put themselves to sleep" for the middle. Similarly, for the optimist, the positive outcomes of any given course of action are especially salient or strongly connected to elements of the environment, and vice versa with negative outcomes for the pessimist, so then we find both systematically over-construe the positives or negatives of a particular act respectively relative to what actually eventuates.

6.6 Hypothesis filtering and preference for confirmation as cognitive dissonance

Two well known regularities in thought are the phenomena known as "hypothesis filtering" and "preference for confirmation". These phenomena (Rabin, 1998) are actually the same phenomena viewed from different perspectives. Hypothesis filtering exists when the individual i "filters" apparent relations $R_{hh'} \in \rho\ (v_N)$ between the objects of reality based on whether or not they are consistent with their view of the world, those which are inconsistent being more likely to be rejected.

Definition 31. Hypothesis filtering exists in a particular environment v_N if an individual is more likely to reject any relations $R_{hh'} \in \rho\ (v_N)$ which contradict relations contained within $g(H')$, where $H' \subset \rho\ (v_N)$, than those which do not.

Preference for confirmation exists when the individual seeks, or prefers, to incorporate relations $R_{hh'} \in \rho\ (v_N)$ which do not contradict their view of the world.

Definition 32. Preference for confirmation exists in a particular environment v_N if an individual is more likely to accept any relations $R_{hh'} \in \rho\ (v_N)$ which do not contradict relations contained within $g(H')$, where $H' \subset \rho\ (v_N)$, than those which do.

We can demonstrate with relative ease that these two phenomena are actually manifestations of a more fundamental resistance to cognitive dissonance.

Theorem 18 (Cognitive dissonance implies hypothesis testing and preference for confirmation). *If the law of resistance to dissonance (definition 16) holds, then the individual will display hypothesis filtering and preference for confirmation.*

This does not mean that we will always be resistant to every idea that contradicts our world view $g(H)$. Quite apart from the possibility of acceptance introduced if it is the case that $p(R_{hh'} \in g(H)) > 0$, dissonance only exists, and the discomfort attendant upon it, if there are contradictory relations $R_{hh'} \in g(H')$ in the individual's understanding of the particular situation which gives rise to $g(H')$. It is possible that relations $R_{hh'} \in \rho\ (v_N)$ which contradict an individual's understanding of the world $g(H)$ are incorporated nonetheless because in the particular environment v_N it was apparent there were few if any contradictory relations contained within the understanding $g(H')$ of it. An individual is more likely to incorporate apparent relations between their nicotine use and their chances of developing cancer if they are not enjoying a cigarette and experiencing the pleasant relaxation attendant upon it.

6.7 Made to stick: why certain ideas are more likely to be accepted

We might complete our discussion of the behavioural and psychological phenomena explained and predicted by the theory developed in this work by a discussion of how it contains an explanation of the six factors proposed by Heath and Heath (2007) (a significant, if rather "pop" contribution) governing whether an idea will be accepted or not, assented to, and incorporated into the individual's worldview. In their words, these factors explain why some ideas "stick" when others do not.

Definition 33 (An idea). *A proposed idea is a set $\{R_{hh'}\}^P$ of connections between percepts h,h' of the objects of reality.*

Theorem 19 (When ideas are "made to stick"). *Suppose, in addition to the theory hitherto developed, that the individual's perception, $\rho\ (\cdot)$, has the salience property 6.4, and the likelihood $p(\cdot)$ of the incorporation of relations $R_{hh'}$ can be extended to map sets of relations. The likelihood of any proposed idea $\{R_{hh'}\}^P$ being incorporated into the mind of the individual, $p(\{R_{hh'}\}^P \subset g(H))$ in the particular environment v_N is*

1   *Decreasing in the number of relations $|\{R_{hh'}\}^P|$ the idea contains:*

$$\frac{\partial p(\{R_{hh'}\}^P \subset g(H))}{\partial |\{R_{hh'}\}^P|} \le 0 \tag{6.11}$$

2   *Increasing in the number of relations in the idea already incorporated in the individual's mind, $|R_{hh'} \in \{R_{hh'}\}^P : R_{hh'} \in g(H)|$:*

$$\frac{\partial p(\{R_{hh'}\}^P \subset g(H))}{\partial |R_{hh'} \in \{R_{hh'}\}^P : R_{hh'} \in g(H)|} \geq 0 \qquad (6.12)$$

3   *Increasing in the relative noticeability $\sigma(v') - \sigma(v_N)$ of the information $v' \in 2^{v_N} : h = \rho(v')$ which corresponds to the percept h for each of the objects or events h related by any individual relation in the idea $R_{hh'} \in \{R_{hh'}\}^P$*

$$\frac{\partial p(\{R_{hh'}\}^P \subset g(H))}{\partial [\sigma(v') - \sigma(v_N)]} \geq 0 \, \forall \, v' \in 2^{v_N} : h = \rho(v') \, \& \, R_{hh'} \in \{R_{hh'}\}^P$$

4   *Decreasing in the dissonance of each individual relation in the idea $R_{hh'} \in \{R_{hh'}\}^P$:*

$$\frac{\partial p(\{R_{hh'}\}^P \subset g(H))}{\partial |\{R_{h''h'''} \in g(H') : R_{hh'} \Rightarrow \neg R_{h''h'''}\}|} \geq 0 \, \forall \, R_{hh'} \in \{R_{hh'}\}^P \qquad (6.13)$$

where $|\{R_{h''h'''} \in g(H') : R_{hh'} \Rightarrow \neg R_{h''h'''}\}|$ is the number of relations in $g(H')$ the relation $R_{hh'} \in \{R_{hh'}\}^P$ is dissonant with.

5   *Decreasing in the centrality $c(C_{g(H)}(h) \quad C_{g(H)}(h'))$ within the system of personal constructs, $g(H)$, of each individual relation $R_{hh'} \in \{R_{hh'}\}^P$ in the idea:*

$$\frac{\partial p(\{R_{hh'}\}^P \subset g(H))}{\partial c\left(C_{g(H)}(h) \quad C_{g(H)}(h')\right)} \geq 0 \, \forall \, R_{hh'} \in \{R_{hh'}\}^P \qquad (6.14)$$

where $c(\cdot)$ is some combination of the network centralities $C_{g(H)}(h)$ and $C_{g(H)}(h')$.

The Heath brothers suggest six factors in the problem of making an idea "stick", summarised by the jaunty acronym S.U.C.C.E.S. An idea that is Simple, that is Unexpected, that is Concrete, that is Credible, that is Emotional, and that is told as a Story is more likely to be incorporated than an idea that is not. Theorem 19 reduces these to four deep factors and indicates a fifth not originally included in the factors of S.U.C.C.E.S.

Property 1 is straightforward: the more connections one must make in order to incorporate an idea into one's mind the more unlikely that idea is to be incorporated as a whole. That is, an idea must be simple. Property 2 indicates that the more connections in an idea which are already included in the mind of the individual, the more likely the idea is to be incorporated wholesale. This, interpreted a little further, suggests that an idea which can be formed fully by the addition of a few relations between ideas already existing in the mind is far more likely than an idea that must be introduced wholesale. The brothers Heath speak of this as "concreteness"; if an idea can be formed by the making of a few connections which "latch on" to existing knowledge, it is "concrete" – not something we are completely unaware of *a priori* – and thus something we are more likely to incorporate into our world-view.

Now we come again to the notion of salience in property 3. Unless the elements to be related together by the idea are salient enough relative to the environment to actually be perceived, there is little chance the idea which relates those elements is going to be assented to. Nothing is more noticeable than the unexpected, and the very connotations of the word "visceral" suggest emotions, needs, desires are highly salient relative to their environment. Hence we reduce two of the Heath's factors – unexpectedness and emotional content – to one: salience. If an idea engages our emotions, if it is unexpected, then it stands out and is that much more likely to be noticed and thus understood.

But there is nuance (noticed also by Heath and Heath, 2007), for ideas which are unexpected and emotional may well be highly cognitively dissonant, and cause significant discomfort if incorporated. Property 4 dictates ideas which are cognitively dissonant with the understanding $g(H')$ of the situation at hand are less likely to be incorporated into the understanding $g(H)$. Note the further nuance, that if any relations dissonant with the idea in $g(H)$ are not elicited in the understanding $g(H')$ of the particular situation, they are not counted as dissonant with the idea and do not lessen the likelihood of its incorporation. But an idea, if not carefully constructed so as to be unusual without being "outlandish" and presented in the "right" context, is as easily able to elicit a negative response than a positive – unexpected ideas, and ideas which contradict our desires and emotional needs, are uncomfortable, thus less likely to be incorporated.

Property 4 in addition to placing nuance on the factors of unexpectedness and emotional content, also relates closely to the Heath condition of credibility. To assent to, to believe, an idea from a non-credible source is literally contradictory. Credibility is literally related to the notion of belief by its very etymology. The more credible the source of an idea to the minds of the individual in question, the more likely that idea is to be consonant with their understanding of a particular environment, and the more likely it is to be accepted. This is, however, fickle, for the dissonance in accepting, believing an idea from a non-credible, non-believable source is contingent on the *individual's* belief of credibility, which is not necessarily the same as others.

If we push property 4 even further, we see that it is a mathematical demonstration of the importance of telling good stories, the final factor the Heath brothers identify. A story is a progression of events, which have some logic to them in the sense of "flow"; it is the more memorable because each point in a good story leads to the next. In the financial markets in particular, we tell ourselves stories in order to weave incoherent data into an understandable idea of which we may be more convinced (Akerlof and Shiller, 2009; Shiller, 2017). A "good" story is one that doesn't contain "deep" contradictions, each step $R_{hh'}$ in the story progresses in a non-contradictory way from the previous step. The less "intuitive" a progression of events within an idea $\{R_{hh'}\}^P$, the more dissonance that exists in that progression, the less likely each subsequent step within the idea is to be incorporated.

The major potential objections to this argument are the *deus ex machina* and "plot-twist" principles of literary theory. But far from outlawing them, theorem 19 actually makes sense of why these "breakpoints" in a story are memorable. They are salient (condition 3), and, in the context of the "plot-twist", will also in retrospect be consonant with the rest of the story (condition 4), hence the plot twist in particular is such an excellent literary device for creating a memorable story.[5]

Finally, property 5 is a demonstration of a fairly intuitive fact: the more an idea tries to pose ideas that change the core of "who people are", which change the core of the way they understand the world, the more resistance that idea is going to encounter. There is an underlying degree of constancy in our psychology. Our view of the world might indeed change radically quite suddenly, but this only comes about through changes in individual relations, at the margins of how we think about the world.

Notes

1. Rick and Loewenstein (2008) make a useful and instructive distinction between the "tangible" present, and the "intangible" outcomes of the future which means only the visceral, noticeable emotions construed of the future are likely to be at play in decision making.
2. Note that the follow-on property also interacts with the salience property in the form the latter is specified. If the follow-on property is satisfied for some percepts h and h' and a connection $R_{hh'}$, then the latter percept, h' must be sufficiently salient to be perceived. This is because, to follow the mathematics, from equation 6.5, $h \in H'$ & $\exists R_{hh'} \in g(H) : s(R_{hh'}) - \sigma(v_N) \geq \bar{s} \Rightarrow h' \in H'$ and therefore from equation 6.4 we have that $\sigma(v') - \sigma(v_N) \geq \bar{\sigma}$ for that v : $h' = \rho(v)$.

3. Formally, the generalisation would be

$$\{h_n\}_{n \in N} \subset H' \ \& \ \exists \{R_{h_n h'}\}_{n \in N} \subset g(H) : \sum_{n \in N} s(R_{h_n h'})$$
$$\geq \sigma(v_N) + \bar{s} \Rightarrow h' \in H'$$

(6.15)

where $\sum_{n \in N}$ is a summation with respect to the index n.

4. See the talk given by Ariely in 2008, "Are we in control of our own decisions?", available at URL: https://www.ted.com/talks/dan_ariely_asks_are_-we_in_ control_of_our_own_decisions?language=en

5. We all (who have read the *Lord of the Rings* and the *Hobbit*) remember "the eagles are coming", for it is arguably the most stunning *deus ex machina* in literature, used by Tolkien to get his characters out of impossible situations. It is totally incongruent with the general flow of otherwise exceptionally well crafted and written plots and thus highly noticeable. Similarly, the author, for instance, can't remember much of the *Half Blood Prince*, still less of *The Deathly Hallows*; for all that he loved J. K. Rowling's writing, he found them decidedly lacking in structure and economy, but he most surely can remember the plot twist of Albus Dumbledore being killed. Rowling's character had hitherto been omnipresent and designed to be well-loved for his stable and calming presence and thus his death, totally incongruent with his place in the plot up to that point, was hugely salient in the mind of the reader. The general flow of the *Harry Potter* narrative still tends to be a highly "sticky" idea though fraying a little toward its end, for each of these plot twists (several other prominent characters are killed throughout the course of the series) are revealed by Rowling's storytelling to fit well in the flow of the story *ex post*.

References

Ainslie, G., 1986. *The Multiple Self.* Cambridge University Press, Cambridge, Ch. Beyond microeconomics, conflict among interests in a multiple self as a determinant of value, pp. 133–175.

Akerlof, G., Shiller, R., 2009. *Animal Spirits.* Princeton University Press, Princeton.

Ariely, D., 2008. *Predictably Irrational.* Harper Perennial, New York.

Baddeley, M., 2010. Herding, social influence and economic decision-making: socio-psychological and neuroscientific analyses. *Philosophical Transactions of the Royal Society B* 365, 281–290.

Baddeley, M., 2013. Herding, social influence and expert opinion. *Journal of Economic Methodology* 20 (1), 35–44.

Baddeley, M., 2015. Herding, social influences and behavioural bias in scientific research. *EMBO Reports* 16 (8), 902–905.

Barberis, N., 2013. Thirty years of prospect theory in economics. *Journal of Economic Perspectives* 27 (1), 173–196.

Becker, G., 1962. Irrational behavior and economic theory. *Journal of Political Economy* 70 (1), 1–13.

Bergson, H., 1946. *The Creative Mind.* Citadel Press, New York.

Clark, A., Frijters, P., Shields, M., 2008. Relative income, happiness and utility: An explanation for the Easterlin paradox and other puzzles. *Journal of Economic Literature* 46 (1), 95–144.

Duesenberry, J., 1949. *Income, Saving, and the Theory of Consumer Behavior.* Harvard University Press, Cambridge, MA.

Earl, P., 2015. Anchoring in economics: On Frey and Gallus on the aggregation of behavioural anomalies. *Economics* 9. Available at URL: http://dx.doi.org/10.5018/economics-ejournal.ja.2015-21

Easterlin, R., 2001. Income and happiness: Toward a unified theory. *Economic Journal* 111, 465–484.

Elster, J., 1986. *The Multiple Self.* Cambridge University Press, Cambridge.

Elster, J., 1998. Emotions and economic theory. *Journal of Economic Literature* 36 (1), 47–74.

Frank, R., 2011. *The Darwin Economy.* Princeton University Press, Princeton.

Frederick, S., Loewenstein, G., O'Donoghue, T., 2002. Time discounting and time preference: A critical review. *Journal of Economic Literature* XL, 351–401.

Galbraith, J., 1958. *The Affluent Society.* Penguin, London.

Hayek, F., 1952. *The Sensory Order.* University of Chicago Press, Chicago.

Heath, C., Heath, D., 2007. *Made to Stick.* Random House, New York.

Hinkle, D., 1965. *The Change of Personal Constructs From the Viewpoint of a Theory of Construct Implications.* Doctoral dissertation, Ohio State University.

Hirsch, F., 1977. *The Social Limits to Growth.* Routledge, London.

Hume, D., 1777. *An Enquiry Concerning Human Understanding*, 2nd Edition. Hackett Publishing Company, Cambridge.

Kahneman, D., 2003. Maps of bounded rationality: Psychology for behavioural economics. *American Economic Review* 93 (5), 1449–1475.

Kahneman, D., Thaler, R., 2006. Anomalies: Utility maximization and experienced utility. *Journal of Economic Perspectives* 20 (1), 221–234.

Kahneman, D., Tversky, A., 1979. Prospect theory: An analysis of decision under risk. *Econometrica* 47 (2), 263–292.

Kandel, E., Schwartz, J., Jessell, T., Siegelbaum, S., Hudspeth, A. (Eds.), 2013. *Principles of Neural Science*, 5th Edition. McGraw-Hill, New York.

Kelly, G., 1963. *A Theory of Personality.* Norton, New York.

Layard, R., 2011. *Happiness*, revised Edition. Penguin, New York.

Loewenstein, G., 1996. Out of control: Visceral influence on behavior. *Organizational Behavior and Human Decision Processes* 65 (3), 272–292.

Loewenstein, G., 2000. Emotions in economic theory and economic behavior. *American Economic Review* 90 (2), 426–432.

Mehta, J., 2013. The discourse of bounded rationality in academic and policy arenas: pathologising the errant consumer. *Cambridge Journal of Economics* 37, 1243–1261.

Packard, V., 1957. *The Hidden Persuaders.* Pelican, London.

Rabin, M., 1998. Psychology and economics. *Journal of Economic Literature* 36 (1), 11–46.

Rabin, M., 2013a. An approach to incorporating psychology into economics. *American Economic Review* 103 (3), 617–622.

Rabin, M., 2013b. Incorporating limited rationality into economics. *Journal of Economic Literature* 51 (2), 528–543.

Rick, S., Loewenstein, G., 2008. Intangibility in intertemporal choice. *Philosophical Transactions of the Royal Society B* 363, 3813–3824.

Rorty, A., 1986. *The Multiple Self.* Cambridge University Press, Cambridge, Ch. Self-deception, akrasia and irrationality, pp. 115–131.

Sapolsky, R., 2017. *Behave.* Penguin, London.

Shiller, R., 2017. *Narrative Economics.* Cowles Foundation Discussion Paper No. 2069.

Simon, H., 1947. *Administrative Behavior*, 4th Edition. The Free Press, New York.

Taleb, N., 2007. *The Black Swan.* Penguin, London.

Thaler, R., 1980. Toward a positive theory of consumer choice. Journal of Economic *Behavior and Organization* 1, 39–60.

Thaler, R., Sunstein, C., 2008. *Nudge.* Yale University Press, New Haven.

Tierney, J., Bauermeister, R., 2011. *Willpower.* Penguin, London.

Tversky, A., Kahneman, D., 1974. Judgment under uncertainty: Heuristics and biases. *Science* 185 (4157), 1124–1131.

Tversky, A., Kahneman, D., 1981. The framing of decisions and the psychology of choice. *Science* 211 (4481), 453–458.

Veblen, T., 1898. Why is economics not an evolutionary science? *Quarterly Journal of Economics* 12 (4), 373–397.

Veblen, T., 1899. *The Theory of the Leisure Class.* Oxford University Press, Oxford World's Classics.

Vernon, M., 1962. *The Psychology of Perception.* Pelican, London.

7 Conclusion

The present work has proposed an integrated, holistic and systematic theory of our lived experience, and offered a psychological foundation for the Science of Everyday Life thereby. It is simple and coherent while also being comprehensive and rigorous. The theory was developed from the proposition that the mind is a network structure within which and upon which the psychological process operates. By way of conclusion, let us briefly reconsider the theory we have developed and then the manner in which this work is but the beginning of a new, useful science of ourselves, our place in the world and our interaction with it.

7.1 A summary of our theory

The theory of psychology and behaviour we have proposed is, when stripped of auxiliary considerations and stated in essence alone, actually quite simple. We perceive the objects and events in our environment and any apparent relations between them (definition 5):

$$\{H' \quad \{R_{hh'}\}\} = \rho\left(v_{N(g)}\right) \tag{7.1}$$

We form an analysis of that environment based on the relations $g(H)$ we construed between the objects and events in our world (definition 7):

$$g(H') = \{R_{hh'} \in g(H) : h, h' \in H'\} \subset g(H) \tag{7.2}$$

We theorise (theorem 2) that we make choices among feasible actions $a \in B$ available to us based on the preferability of implications implied by the language in which understanding $g(H')$ is expressed:

$$a^* = \{a \in B : g_a \succ g_{a'} \, \forall a' \in B\} \tag{7.3}$$

where g_a are the implications of selecting action a (definition 10), and $B \subset 2^{A'}$ is the set of feasible actions. The basis of this decision, our personal knowledge of the world $g(H)$, evolves over time by the incorporation of new connections and the fading into irrelevance of the old.

Notwithstanding its basic simplicity, the formalism of which these three objects are essential demonstrates that despite their otherwise unfathomably complex and individuated nature, we may observe there to be a relatively simple, even elegant structure common to their outward form, an architecture of mind. It contains two major approaches to the psychology of the individual: the psychology of picture-linguistic thinking and the psychology of decision rules. It permits social factors to influence psychology and behaviour. It demonstrates, furthermore, that many of the observed phenomena of behaviour are not particular and disconnected, but rather it explains and predicts them as natural aspects of a common structure to thought and decision making.

7.2 Future directions for the Science of Everyday Life

The theory presented here constitutes not an end but a beginning. It offers a foundation for a Science of Everyday Life, a basic theory of our lived experience. There is much to be done to build this science before it can be considered at all satisfactory.

There is much to be done even with respect to psychology. The work of one (young) man, this book has necessarily touched very lightly on what is a vast literature reporting and exploring the phenomena of the human psyche. Only a few of the tens of "biases and heuristics" in the currently popular literature, and still fewer of the hundreds of psycho-behavioural phenomena in the literature of psychological science more broadly, have been integrated within the rubric of the present theory. That is in large part because while we have approached the fundamental aspects of the psyche in a systematic manner, we have largely considered them in isolation and not used their interaction to build theories of more complex psychological and behavioural phenomena. There is much to be done to rectify this failing of the present work, to take the theory it proposes and by applying it integrate within it a far greater set of phenomena than have been approached here. Integrating the present theory with each heuristic and complex psycho-behavioural phenomenon discovered and explored in the psychological literature more broadly really deserves its own academic paper.

In particular, one set of phenomena it would be very interesting to approach with the theory proposed here is the set of psychopathologies.

The manner in which neuroses and psychoses exist as mental states, how they are elicited, how they affect thinking and behaviour and how they may be alleviated are questions which might be approached in a more integrated, holistic and systematic manner than has hitherto been possible. Life includes pathologies, so a vital direction for the Science of Everyday Life to take in the future is to give an account of such pathologies.

As important a direction for the Science of Everyday Life to take is to extend the foundation presented here toward a more explicit theory of society and social interaction. The Science of Everyday Life must contain an account of how individuals interact for it is such a defining characteristic of our existence. The present work offers a foundation for such a theory in the explanation it offers of how the world interacts with individual psychology and behaviour.

If we apply the theory of psychology presented here to, say, the behaviour of an individual as a node in a social network in the style of models proposed by Bonaichi and Lee (2012), Borgatti et al. (2009), Jackson and Watts (2002), Jackson (2008) and Watts (2004), we would discover a new theory of society and social interaction built from an integrated, holistic and systematic theory of how individuals respond to their world and act in it on the basis of their psychology. All that is necessary to obtain such a theory from a logico-mathematical perspective is to be explicit about the environment of the individual containing information communicated within social networks, and the manner in which the individual's actions create connections in social networks. Such an endeavour regarding, specifically, *economic* networks and a theory of the *economy* as a part of social systems has already been explored at the University of Queensland, Australia (see the technical document Markey-Towler, 2016).

The present theory is useful in the sense that it offers us an integrated, holistic and systematic perspective on the human mind, psychology and behaviour which is intellectually competitive with the view proposed by neoclassical economics (Harstad and Selten, 2013). It offers a simple, coherent yet also comprehensive and rigorous approach which allows us to understand the psychological process and behaviour which arises from it. It is especially interdisciplinary insofar as it develops foundations firmly placed within the psychological literature for what is called behavioural economics, which is of significant interest for practical minded strategists in industry and policymakers in the government seeking to induce behavioural change.

If the reader might permit me to stray just once briefly into political matters in conclusion, I would caution the reader to seriously consider the ethics of seeking to induce behavioural change by means of manipulating the environment and thus the psychological process. Mario Rizzo

(Rizzo and Whitman, 2009; Rizzo, 2009; Whitman and Rizzo, 2007, 2015) has written forcefully on this subject. Such interventions must betray the belief of the policymaker that their personal knowledge of the world, their ethics and their morality expressed therein is of a superior kind. Stripped of all niceties and subtleties, interventions aimed at inducing behavioural change other than by open argument and persuasion in the process of public reasoning betray an ambition by the one to impose their worldview on another. The liberal *ethos* rebels deeply against such actions, especially on the part of a government equipped with the means of violent coercion. The challenge posed by the classical texts of Sir Karl Popper (1945) and John Stuart Mill (1895) must always be risen to by those who would seek to use the power of the state for social engineering, lest they reveal what must otherwise be the arrogance and brutality of the authoritarian or totalitarian mindset.

There lies the psychological foundation of the Science of Everyday Life, and some potential directions for its future development. At least as I see it. I've found the theory proposed here immensely useful for understanding myself, others and our place in the world. I hope you will feel similarly. And I hope therefore that it provides you with some of the joy of knowledge it has provided me and that only the ring of some sort of truth (however small) can provide.

Magna est veritas et prevalebit

References

Bonaichi, P., Lee, P., 2012. *Introduction to Mathematical Sociology*. Princeton University Press, Princeton.

Borgatti, S., Mehra, A., Brass, D., Labianca, G., 2009. Network analysis in the social sciences. *Science* 323, 892–895.

Harstad, R., Selten, R., 2013. Bounded-rationality models: Tasks to become intellectually competitive. *Journal of Economic Literature* 51 (2), 496–511.

Jackson, M., 2008. *Social and Economic Networks*. Princeton University Press, Princeton.

Jackson, M., Watts, A., 2002. The evolution of social and economic networks. *Journal of Economic Theory* 106 (2), 265–395.

Markey-Towler, B., 2016. *Foundations for Economic Analysis: The Architecture of Socioeconomic Complexity*. PhD thesis, School of Economics, The University of Queensland, available at URL: http://dx.doi.org/10.14264/uql.2017.91

Mill, J., 1859. *On Liberty*. Penguin, London.

Popper, K., 1945. *The Open Society and Its Enemies*. Routledge, London.

Rizzo, M., 2009. Little brother is watching you: New paternalism on the slippery slopes. *Arizona Law Review* 51 (685), 685–739.

98   *Conclusion*

Rizzo, M., Whitman, D., 2009. The knowledge problem of the new paternalism. *Brigham Young University Law Review* 2009 (4), 905–968.
Watts, D., 2004. The "new" science of networks. *Annual Review of Sociology* 30, 243–270.
Whitman, D., Rizzo, M., 2007. Paternalist slopes. *NYU Journal of Law and Liberty* 2 (411), 411–443.
Whitman, D., Rizzo, M., 2015. The problematic welfare standards of behavioural paternalism. *Review of Philosophy and Psychology* 6 (3), 409–425.

8 Appendix

Proofs of theorems

Proof of corollary 1: Acts contain objects of reality

Proof. By definition 9, $a^* = \rho\left(v_N^{a^*}\right) \cap A'$. So if $a^* \neq \emptyset$ it must therefore either be the case since $A' = \rho\left(v_N^a \subset v_N\right) \cap \{H' \quad g(H')\}$ (equation 3.5) and $\rho\left(v_N^{a^*}\right) \subset \rho\left(v_N^a \subset v_N\right) \subset \{H' \quad \{R_{hh'}\}\}$ (definitions 5 and 6) that either $\exists h \in a^*$, or $\exists R_{hh'} \in a^*$. But similarly by that definition, if the latter is the case, $R_{hh'} \in \rho\left(v_N^{a^*}\right) \Rightarrow h, h' \in \rho\left(v_N^{a^*}\right)$, hence we can conclude that if $\exists R_{hh'} \in a^* = \rho\left(v_N^{a^*}\right) \cap A' \subset \rho\left(v_N^{a^*}\right)$, then $\exists h \in \rho\left(v_N^{a^*}\right)$. Now since $\rho\left(v_N^{a^*}\right) \subset \rho\left(v_N^a \subset v_N\right)$ by definition 9 it must be that $h \in \rho\left(v_N^a \subset v_N\right)$, and by definition 6, $\rho\left(v_N^a \subset v_N\right) \subset \rho(v_N) = \{H' \quad \{R_{hh'}\}\}$, so we must have $h \in \rho(v_N)\backslash\{R_{hh'}\} = H'$. By equation 3.5, then $h \in \rho\left(v_N^a \subset v_N\right)$ and $h \in H'$, so $h \in A'$. Then we can conclude that since $h \in \rho\left(v_N^{a^*}\right)$ and $h \in A'$, we have $h \in a^*$.

Proof of theorem 1: Existence of acts and behavioural mappings

Proof. 1. If an individual is to engage in a particular environment, that is, $\exists v_N^{a^*} \subset v_N$ then there must be perception of it, that is, $\rho\left(v_N^{a^*}\right) \neq \emptyset$. Since by definition 9, this perception must be contained within perceptions of the potential behaviour in that particular environment we can conclude that

$$\rho\left(v_N^{a^*}\right) \subset \rho\left(v_N^a \subset v_N\right) \Rightarrow \rho\left(v_N^a \subset v_N\right) \neq \emptyset \tag{8.1}$$

By definition 6, $R_{hh'} \in \rho\left(v_N^a \subset v_N\right) \neq \emptyset \Rightarrow h, h' \in \rho\left(v_N^a \subset v_N\right)$, so we can conclude that

$$\exists h \in \rho\left(v_N^a \subset v_N\right) \tag{8.2}$$

Now since by definition 6 $\rho\left(v_N^a \subset v_N\right) = \rho\left(v_N^a\right) \cap \rho(v_N)$ and therefore $\rho\left(v_N^a \subset v_N\right) \subset \rho(v_N)$, we can further conclude that

$$\exists h \in \rho\left(v_N^a \subset v_N\right) \Rightarrow h \in \rho(v_N) \tag{8.3}$$

and since $\rho(v_N) = \{H' \quad \{R_{hh'}\}\}$, we can conclude $h \in \{H'\} \subset \{R_{hh'}\}$ also, and thus that $h \in \rho\left(v_N^a \subset v_N\right) \cap \{H' \quad g(H_i')\}$. This allows us to conclude then by definition 9 not only that

$$h \in \rho\left(v_N^a \subset v_N\right) \cap \{H' \quad g(H')\} = A' \Rightarrow A' \neq \emptyset \tag{8.4}$$

but since $h \in \{H'\} \subset \{R_{hh'}\}$ also that $h \in A'$ and $h \in H'$, thus $A' \cap H' \neq \emptyset$. Now since by definition 9, $A \supset A'$ and by definition 5 $H \supset H'$, we have that $A' \cap H' \subset A \cap H'$ and $A' \cap H' \subset A \cap H$ and therefore that

$$A' \cap H' \neq \emptyset \Rightarrow A \cap H' \neq \emptyset \tag{8.5}$$

$$A' \cap H' \neq \emptyset \Rightarrow A \cap H \neq \emptyset \tag{8.6}$$

2. If an individual's behaviour is to be $v_N^{a^*} \subset v_N^a \subset v_N \subset V_N$ then there must exist a mapping assigning elements of the environment $v_N \subset V_N$ to the set $v_N^{a^*}$. Since the behaviour and environment are picked arbitrarily, if an individual is to act, there must exist a single-valued mapping $d_v : V_N \rightarrow 2^{V_a}$ to subsets $v_N^{a^*} = d_v(v_N)$ of 2^{V_a} which is well defined for any situation in which $\exists v_N^{a^*} \subset v_N$. But by assumption an individual cannot behave in this manner without perceiving the behaviour, $\rho\left(v_N^{a^*}\right) = \emptyset \Rightarrow \not\exists v_N^{a^*} \subset v_N$, so if $\exists v_N^{a^*} \subset v_N$, it must be the case that $\rho\left(v_N^{a^*}\right) \neq \emptyset$. Now by definition 9 if perception $\rho\left(v_N^{a^*}\right) \subset \rho\left(v_N^a \subset v_N\right)$ of the realised behaviour $v_N^{a^*}$ of the individual contains an apparent relation $R_{hh'}$ between objects of reality it must also include those objects of reality, that is $R_{hh'} \in \rho\left(v_N^{a^*}\right) \Rightarrow h, h' \in \rho\left(v_N^{a^*}\right)$. We can conclude therefore from $\rho\left(v_N^{a^*}\right) \neq \emptyset$ that either $\exists h \in \rho\left(v_N^{a^*}\right)$ or $\exists R_{hh'} \in \rho\left(v_N^{a^*}\right)$, but in the latter case we must anyway have $h \in \rho\left(v_N^{a^*}\right)$. Now by definition 9, specifically 3.5, $A' = \rho\left(v_N^a \subset v_N\right) \cap \{H' \quad g(H')\}$. Since $h \in \rho\left(v_N^{a^*}\right) \subset \rho\left(v_N^a \subset v_N\right)$, we have that $h \in \rho\left(v_N^a \subset v_N\right)$, and further, since by definition 6 $\rho\left(v_N^a \subset v_N\right) \subset \rho(v_N)$ and by definition $5\rho(v_N) = \{H' \quad \{R_{hh'}\}\}$, we must have $h \in \{H' \quad \{R_{hh'}\}\}$, specifically $h \in H'$. Thus as $h \in \rho\left(v_N^a \subset v_N\right)$ and $h \in H'$, we have $h \in A'$. So we have that $h \in \rho\left(v_N^{a^*}\right)$ and $h \in A'$ and hence we can conclude that

$$a^* = \rho\left(v_N^{a^*}\right) \cap A' \neq \emptyset \tag{8.7}$$

So the perception mapping $\rho : V_N \rightarrow \{H \cup R\}$ implies there is a mapping $\rho^a \subset \rho$ within perception ρ which maps behaviour $v_N^{a^*} = d_v(v_N)$ contained within 2^{V_a} to those actions, $a^* = \rho\left(v_N^{a^*}\right) \cap A'$ which, since $\rho\left(v_N^{a^*}\right) \cap A' \subset A'$

by definition 9 are subsets of A' are subsets of 2^A. So $\exists \rho^a : 2^{V_a} \to 2^A$ which is well defined for any situation in which $\exists v_N^{a^*} \subset v_N$.

Now, $\exists d_v : V_N \to 2^{V_a}$ assigning elements of the particular environment v_N to subsets v_a^* and $\exists \rho^a : 2^{V_a} \to 2^A$ allocating elements of the subsets $v_N^{a^*}$ to act a^*, implies that there exists a mapping d (a composite of the two) assigning elements of the particular environment v_N to behaviour a^*, that is, $\exists d : V_N \to 2^A$. Furthermore, this mapping must be single-valued in 2^A, because if there is to exist behaviour $v_N^{a^*}$, only that information may be perceived as behaviour, $a^* = \rho\left(v_N^{a^*}\right) \cap A' \in d$ and not some other behaviour v_a', so if $a^* = \rho\left(v_N^{a^*}\right) \cap A' \in d$ then $a' = \rho\left(v_a'\right) \notin d$.

Proof of theorem 2: The Theory of Choice

Proof. 1. $(a^* \subset \{a \in B : g_a \succ g_{a'} \ \forall a' \in B\})$: An act a which is associated with the set of implications g_a able to be ranked against any the implications associated with any other feasible actions and which is not less preferable than the implications associated with any other feasible actions is by definition 12 an act $a : g_a \not\succ g_a \forall a' \in B$. Since by definition 12 again $g_{a'} \not\succ g_a \Rightarrow g_{a'} \not\succ g_a \forall a' \in B$, and the implications of any such act a must be able to be ranked against those of any other feasible act, any such act is an act $a : g_a \succ g_{a'} \forall a_a' \in B$. Since a_a^* is an act $a : g_{a'} \not\succ g_a \forall a' \in B$, therefore by definition $a^* = a : g_a \succ g_{a'} \forall a' \in B$. Furthermore the act $a^* \in 2^A$ which the individual selects must be feasible, so by definition 11 it must be the case that $a^* \in B$ and $a^* = a : g_a \succ g_{a'} \forall a' \in B$. This establishes that $a^* \subset \{a \in B : g_a \succ g_{a'} \forall a' \in B\}$.

2. $(a^* \supset \{a \in B : g_a \succ g_{a'} \forall a' \in B\})$: Take an act $a \in B : g_a \succ g_{a'} \forall a' \in B$. The implications of any such action must by its definition be able to be ranked against any the implications associated with any other feasible actions. So we can conclude by definition 12 that any such act $a \in B : g_a \succ g_{a'} \forall a' \in B$ is an act $a \in B : g_{a'} \not\succ g_a \forall a' \in B$, which again by definition 12 is an act which is not less preferable than the implications associated with any other feasible actions. Further, any such act is by its definition and definition 11 a feasible act. Therefore, any act $a \in B : g_a \succ g_{a'} \forall a' \in B$ is a feasible act which is associated with the set of implications g_a able to be ranked against any implications associated with any other feasible actions and which is not less preferable than the implications associated with any other feasible actions. This is the definition of a^* so we have established that $a^* \supset \{a \in B : g_a \succ g_{a'} \forall a' \in B\}$.

3. We have now established that $a^* \subset \{a \in B : g_a \succ g_{a'} \forall a' \in B\}$ and $a^* \supset \{a \in B : g_a \succ g_{a'} \forall a' \in B\}$. Hence every element within a^* is contained within $\{a \in B : g_a \succ g_{a'} \forall a' \in B\}$, and likewise every element within

$\{a \in B : g_a \succ g_{a'} \; \forall a' \in B\}$ is contained within a^*. Therefore, we can conclude that $a^* = \{a \in B : g_a \succ g_{a'} \; \forall a' \in B\}$.

Proof of theorem 3: The "make up your mind/checkmate" theorem

Proof. Let us assume for the present that the set of feasible actions within the set of available actions in a particular situation is non-empty, that is, $B \subset A' \neq \emptyset$. We can now prove the necessity and sufficiency within this assumption of conditions 2 and 3.

(Sufficiency): If by condition 2 there is an act $a \in B$ for which $\nexists a' \in B : \succeq \circ 2^{g(H)} \not\Rightarrow g_a \succeq g_{a'} \vee g_{a'} \succeq g_a \vee g_a \sim g_{a'}$, then all other potential acts $a' \in B$ can be ranked with respect to a, so either $g_a \succeq g_{a'}$ or $g_{a'} \succeq g_a$ or both, that is $g_a \succeq g_{a'} \vee g_{a'} \succeq g_a \vee g_a \sim g_{a'} \; \forall a' \in B$. Now, if further by condition 3 there is an act $a \in B$ for which $\nexists a' \in B : \succeq \circ 2^{g(H)} \Rightarrow g_{a'} \succeq g_a \; \forall a' \in B$, then it must be the case by definition 12 that $g_a \succeq g_{a'} \; \forall a' \in B$, but that $\nexists a' \in B : g_a \sim g_{a'}$, and so again by definition 12 we have that $g_a \succ g_{a'} \; \forall a' \in B$. Since $a \in B$, $\exists a : a = \{a \in B : g_a \succ g_{a'} \; \forall a' \in B\}$.

(Necessity): Suppose $\exists a : a = \{a \in B : g_a \succ g_{a'} \; \forall a' \in B\}$. But suppose by way of contradiction that there is no $a \in B$ such that 2. $\nexists a' \in B : \succeq \circ 2^{g(H)} \not\Rightarrow g_a \succeq g_{a'} \vee g_{a'} \succeq g_a \vee g_a \sim g_{a'}$ and 3. $\nexists a' \in B : \succeq \circ 2^{g(H)} \Rightarrow g_{a'} \succeq g_a$. In this case, for every $a \in B$ there either $\exists a' \in B : \succeq \circ 2^{g(H)} \Rightarrow g_a \succeq g_{a'} \vee g_{a'} \succeq g_a \vee g_a \sim g_{a'}$ or $\exists a' \in B : \succeq \circ 2^{g(H)} \Rightarrow g_{a'} \succeq g_a$ or both. Take an arbitrary $a \in B$ for which this is true.

Now take the first existence statement. If $\exists a' \in B : \succeq \circ 2^{g(H)} \Rightarrow g_a \succeq g_{a'} \vee g_{a'} \succeq g_a \vee g_a \sim g_{a'}$ we cannot establish that $g_a \succeq g_{a'}$ but not $g_{a'} \succeq g_a$ and so we cannot establish that $g_a \succ g_{a'}$, and so $\exists a' \in B : g_a \not\succ g_{a'}$, and so $a \neq \{a \in B : g_a \succ g_{a'} \; \forall a' \in B\}$. Now take the second existence statement. If $\exists a' \in B : \succeq \circ 2^{g(H)} \Rightarrow g_{a'} \succeq g_a$ then by definition 12 $\exists a' \in B : g_a \not\succ g_{a'}$, and so $a \neq \{a \in B : g_a \succ g_{a'} \; \forall a' \in B\}$. In both cases $\exists a' \in B : g_a \not\succ g_{a'}$, so if both are true then $\exists a' \in B : g_a \not\succ g_{a'}$ and $a \neq \{a \in B : g_a \succ g_{a'} \; \forall a' \in B\}$. Since $a \in B$ was picked arbitrarily, and $a \neq \{a \in B : g_a \succ g_{a'} \; \forall a' \in B\} \; \forall a \in B$, and therefore $\nexists a : a = \left\{a \in B : g_a \succ g_{a'} \; \forall a' \in B\right\}$, which contradicts the statement $\exists a : a = \{a \in B : g_a \succ g_{a'} \; \forall a' \in B\}$.

Finally, let us consider condition 1. Since 2 and 3 imply as demonstrated above that $\exists a : a = \{a \in B : g_a \succ g_{a'} \; \forall a' \in B\}$ when the set $B \subset 2^{A'}$ is presumed to be non-empty, then if $B \subset 2^{A'} \neq \emptyset$ and conditions 2 and 3 hold, then indeed $\exists a : a = \{a \in B : g_a \succ g_{a'} \; \forall a' \in B\}$. Now suppose by way of contradiction that $B \subset 2^{A'} = \emptyset$. In this case, $\nexists a \in B$, and therefore necessarily, in fact trivially, $\nexists a : a = \{a \in B : g_a \succ g_{a'} \forall a' \in B\}$, which contradicts $\exists a : a = \{a \in B : g_a \succ g_{a'} \forall a' \in B\}$. Hence it is necessary for choice to be well-defined that $B \subset 2^{A'} \neq \emptyset$.

Proof of corollary 2: The law of attraction to consonance

Proof. Take the set of relations $R_{h''h'''} \in g(H')$. Concerning the logical implications of a new relation $R_{hh'}$ there are two mutually exclusive cases. For each $R_{h''h''} \in g(H)$ either we have $R_{hh'} \Rightarrow \neg R_{h''h'''}$, or we have $R_{hh'} \not\Rightarrow \neg R_{h''h'''}$ (the latter includes, but is not equivalent to saying $R_{hh'} \Rightarrow R_{h''h'''}$). We have therefore that

$$R_{hh'}\{\Rightarrow \neg R_{h''h'''}\} \vee \{\Rightarrow \neg R_{h''h'''}\} \forall R_{h''h'''} \in g(H) \Rightarrow$$

$$|\{R_{h''h'''} \in g(H')\}| = |\{R_{h''h'''} \in g(H') : R_{hh'} \Rightarrow \neg R_{h''h'''}\}| \qquad (8.8)$$

$$+ |\{R_{h''h'''} \in g(H') : R_{hh'} \not\Rightarrow \neg R_{h''h'''}\}|$$

so

$$|\{R_{h''h'''} \in g(H') : R_{hh'} \Rightarrow \neg R_{h''h'''}\}| = |\{R_{h''h'''} \in g(H')\}|$$

$$- |\{R_{h''h'''} \in g(H') : R_{hh'} \not\Rightarrow \neg R_{h''h'''}\}| \qquad (8.9)$$

Using definition 16 we can now transform equation 3.13 by substituting equation 8.9 we obtain

$$\frac{\partial p(R_{hh'} \in g(H))}{\partial |\{R_{h''h'''} \in g(H')\}| - |\{R_{h''h'''} \in g(H') : R_{hh'} \not\Rightarrow \neg R_{h''h'''}\}|} \leq 0 \quad (8.10)$$

It is fairly obvious that

$$\frac{\partial |\{R_{h''h'''} \in g(H')\}| - |\{R_{h''h'''} \in g(H') : R_{hh'} \not\Rightarrow \neg R_{h''h'''}\}|}{\partial |\{R_{h''h'''} \in g(H') : R_{hh'} \not\Rightarrow \neg R_{h''h'''}\}|} < 0 \quad (8.11)$$

So we may conclude, by multiplying the left hand sides of equations 8.10 and 8.11 that

$$\frac{\partial p(R_{hh'} \in g(H))}{\partial |\{R_{h''h'''} \in g(H')\}| - |\{R_{h''h'''} \in g(H') : R_{hh'} \not\Rightarrow \neg R_{h''h'''}\}|}$$

$$\times \frac{\partial |\{R_{h''h'''} \in g(H')\}| - |\{R_{h''h'''} \in g(H') : R_{hh'} \not\Rightarrow \neg R_{h''h'''}\}|}{\partial |\{R_{h''h'''} \in g(H') : R_{hh'} \not\Rightarrow \neg R_{h''h'''}\}|} \geq 0 \qquad (8.12)$$

cancelling the like terms $\partial |\{R_{h''h'''} \in g(H')\}| - |\{R_{h''h'''} \in g(H') : R_{hh'} / \Rightarrow$

$\neg R_{h''h'''}\}|$ we obtain the law of attraction to consonance

$$\frac{\partial p(R_{hh'} \in g(H))}{\partial|\{R_{h''h'''} \in g(H') : R_{hh'} \not\Rightarrow \neg R_{h''h'''}\}|} \geq 0$$

Proof of theorem 4 and corollary 3: g(H) may express sentence equivalents and rational thoughts

Proof. (Theorem 4): By definition 18 any sentence equivalent of l must be semantically equivalent to l. Therefore, since $l \in L$ expresses a sequential series of relations between two subjects/objects the sentence equivalent $p_1, p_2, \ldots, p_n$ of l must express a sequential series of relations between two subjects/objects also. The simplest sentence $p_1, p_2, \ldots, p_n$ may express may therefore be mapped onto a simple network dyad $hR_{hh'}h'$ where $R_{hh'} \in g(H)$. More complex sentences the sentence equivalent $p_1, p_2, \ldots, p_n$ may express consist of a sequential series of relations which may be mapped to a chain $\{h_k h_{k+1} \in g(H)\}_{k=1}^{K} \subset g(H)$.

(Corollary 3): If a linguistic sentence expressing rational thought must express a series of relations between two subjects/objects then theorem 4 applies and the sentence equivalent of l may be represented by a chain $\{h_k h_{k+1} \in g(H)\}_{k=1}^{K} \subset g(H)$.

Proof of theorem 5: g(H) may express decision rules

Proof. By definition 19 a decision rule is an algorithm, and may be expressed mathematically as a recursion $f_K(f_{K-1}(\ldots f_{K-K}(\cdot)))$ where each individual function $f_k(\cdot) \in \{f_k(\cdot)\}_{k=0}^{K}$ maps the outputs of either the function $f_{k-1}(\cdot)$ or some basic information H_0 into the inputs of either the function $f_{k+1}(\cdot)$ or some terminal information $H_K \in f_K(\cdot)$. Take the first function $f_0(\cdot) \in \{f_k(\cdot)\}_{k=0}^{K}$ in the algorithmic recursion. We can define H_0 upon which this function $f_0(\cdot): H_0 \to H_1$ operates to exist within the set H of percepts of the objects of reality within an individual's environment, $H_0 \subset H$, and the set H_1 into which it outputs as also within percepts of the objects of reality within an individual's environment, $H_1 \subset H$. For each individual input $h_0 \in H_0 \subset H$ we have it mapped to the output $h_1 = f_0(h_0) \in H_1 \subset H$, and we may represent this mapping within a relation $R_{h_0h_1} \supset f_0(h_0)$, which is a relation $h_0h_1 \in g_H(H)$.

If we collect such relations $R_{h_0h_1}$ across $h_0 \in H_0$ we obtain a set of relations $\{h_0h_1\}_{h_0 \in H_0} \subset g_H(H)$ representing the mapping $f_0(\cdot)$ in $g_H(H)$. Similarly, we can take the second function $f_1(\cdot) \in \{f_k(\cdot)\}_{k=0}^{K}$. We can again define H_1 upon which this function operates to exist within the set H, $H_0 \subset H$, and the set H_2 as also within H, $H_2 \subset H$. For each individual input $h_1 \in H_1 \subset H$ we have it mapped to the output $h_2 = f_0(h_0) \in H_1 \subset H$, and can represent this within a relation $R_{h_1 h_2} \supset f_1(h_1)$, which is a relation $h_1 h_2 \in g(H)$. If we collect such relations $R_{h_1 h_2}$ across $h_1 \in H_1$ we obtain a set of relations $\{h_1 h_2\}_{h_1 \in H_1} \subset g(H)$ representing the mapping $f_1(\cdot)$ in $g(H)$. We can continue this process for each $f_k(\cdot)$ in the recursion and collect the resulting set of relations into a set $\left\{\{h_k h_{k+1}\}_{h_k \in H_k} \subset g(H)\right\}_{k=0}^{K}$, or $\left\{\{h_k h_{k+1}\}_{h_k \in H_k}\right\}_{k=0}^{K} \subset g(H)$.

Now, a particular iteration $f_K(f_{K-1}(\ldots f_{K-K}(h_0 \in H_0)))$ of this algorithm maps a particular bit of information $h_0 \in H_0$ backward along the algorithm, and because each step in the recursion is a function, it maps to single values, from $h_1 = f_0(h_0)$ to $h_2 = f_1(h_1)$ and so on until $h_{K+1} = f_K(h_K)$. Using the argument above, each of these steps $h_{k+1} = f_k(h_k)$ in the algorithm can be associated with one relation $h_k h_{k+1} \in \{h_k h_{k+1}\}_{h_k \in H_k} \subset g(H)$. If we extract these we obtain a single chain $\{h_k h_{k+1}\}_{k=0}^{K} \subset g(H)$. Provided that the elements $\{h_k\}_{k=0}^{K+1}$ of these relations are contained within H', $\{h_k\}_{k=0}^{K+1} \in H'$, we know that since $g(H') \subset g(H)$ by definition 7 that their relations are contained within $g(H')$, that is $\{h_k\}_{k=0}^{K+1} \subset H' \Rightarrow \{h_k h_{k+1}\}_{k=0}^{K} \subset g(H')$.

Proof of theorem 6: Rule-determinism in behaviour

Proof. If preferences are rule-trivial with respect to $f_K(\cdot)$, then by definition 20

$$a' \not\subset f_K(\cdot) \Rightarrow g_{a'} \not\succeq g_a \,\forall a \in S[f_K(\cdot)] \tag{8.13}$$

Now we have that $a = S[f_K(\cdot)]$. Therefore it must be the case that $a' \neq S[f_K(\cdot)]\forall a' \neq a$, and so only if $a' \subset a$ can it be the case that $a' \in S[f_K(\cdot)]$. Since we supposed this cannot be the case for any feasible action, $a \not\supset a'\forall a' \in B$, we have therefore, due to rule-triviality that

$$g_{a'} \not\succeq g_a \,\forall a' \in B \tag{8.14}$$

Since, further, by supposition $g_a \succeq g_{a'}\vee g_{a'} \succeq g_a \vee g_a \sim g_{a'}\forall a' \in B$ we may therefore conclude that since we have $g_{a'} \not\succeq g_a\forall a' \in B$ we must have $g_a \succeq g_{a'}\forall a' \in B$ but *not* $g_{a'} \succeq g_a$ and therefore we have that $g_a \succ g_{a'}\forall a' \in B$. Since we supposed that $a \in B$ we therefore have that $a \in B$ and $g_a \succ g_{a'}\forall a' \in B$ and thus by equation 3.7, $a = a^*$.

Proof of theorem 7: The consequences of nihilism

Proof. Suppose, by way of contradiction, that $\exists a' \in B : g_{a'} \cap g_\psi = \emptyset$. Because this negates the necessary condition of the second axiom of the theory of the origins of preference (definition 22), we know that the preferability of $g_{a'}$ cannot be established with respect to any other sets of implications; $g_{a''} \not\succeq g_{a'} \& g_{a'} \not\succeq g_{a''} \forall a'' \in B$. This means that for *every* feasible act $a'' \in B$ there is an action $a' \in B$ for which the preferability of its implications relative to $g_{a''}$ cannot be established. This contradicts necessary condition 2 of theorem 3 and therefore $\not\exists a = a^*$.

Proof of theorem 8: Substitutability causes behavioural change

Proof. Take a. At the descriptor $\delta_{\bar\theta}$ then by its own and by definition 23 we have that

$$g_a^{\delta_{\bar\theta}} \sim g_{a'} \tag{8.15}$$

Now if, as we have supposed, some $\delta_\theta : \theta > \bar\theta$ prevails, then by condition 1 we have that

$$g_a^{\delta_\theta} \not\succeq g_a^{\delta_{\bar\theta}} \tag{8.16}$$

and, further, since g_a is supposed to remain preference-comparable for all δ_θ in the sequence $\{\delta_\theta\}_{\theta=0}^{\Theta}$ we have

$$g_a^{\delta_\theta} \succ g_a^{\delta_{\bar\theta}} \tag{8.17}$$

and, since θ was picked arbitrarily the same is true of all points in the half-space $(\bar\theta, ..., \Theta]$ of the index set $[0, . . ., \Theta]$. Now by condition 2 we have supposed that $\succeq \circ 2^{g(H)}$ remains transitive between any rankings of the implications of a, a' and a''. Thus we may establish that since

$$g_a^{\delta_\theta} \succ g_a^{\delta_{\bar\theta}} \, \forall \theta \in (\bar\theta, ..., \Theta] \tag{8.18}$$

and

$$g_a^{\delta_{\bar\theta}} \sim g_{a'} \tag{8.19}$$

We have that

$$g_a^{\delta_\theta} \succ g_{a'} \, \forall \theta \in (\bar\theta, ..., \Theta] \tag{8.20}$$

By supposition, $\bar{\theta} < \Theta$ and so therefore the half-space $(\bar{\theta}, ..., \Theta]$ is non-empty, $(\bar{\theta}, ..., \Theta] \neq \emptyset$ and $\exists \theta \in (\bar{\theta}, ..., \Theta]$ so that by the relation directly above

$$\exists \delta_\theta : g_a^{\delta_\theta} \succ g_{a'} \tag{8.21}$$

Pick now such a δ_θ. Since $a \in B$ by assumption, all that remains is to show that $g_a^{\delta_\theta} \succ g_{a''} \, \forall a'' \in B$. We initially had that $a' = a^*$, and so by equation 3.7 it was the case that

$$g_{a'} \succ g_{a''} \, \forall a'' \in B \tag{8.22}$$

We supposed in condition 3 that these preference relations are maintained, and so since we established above that $g_a^{\delta_\theta} \succ g_{a'} \, \forall \theta \in (\bar{\theta}, ..., \Theta]$, and we have picked a $\delta_\theta : \theta > \bar{\theta}$ to prevail, we may therefore by the transitivity supposed to hold between rankings of the implications of a and a' and any particular a'' establish that

$$g_a^{\delta_\theta} \succ g_{a''} \, \forall a'' \in B \, \forall \theta \in (\bar{\theta}, ..., \Theta] \tag{8.23}$$

where, to abuse notation we include a' in the set of $a'' \in B$. Therefore, since $a \in B$ by assumption and $g_a \succ g_{a''} \in a'' \in B$, we have $a = a^*$ by equation 3.7 for any $\delta_\theta : \theta > \bar{\theta}$ which prevails.

Proof of theorem 9: Rule triviality implies non-substitutability

Proof. (Non-substitutability): If the course of action a is *not* selected by the decision rule $f_K(\cdot) \subset g(H')$, $a \notin S[f_K(\cdot)] \subset g(H')$ while the course of action a' which *is* selected by the decision rule $f_K(\cdot) \subset g(H')$ then by definition 20 we have that $g_a \not\succeq g_{a'}$. Since the conventional interpretation of the pre-ordering $\succeq \circ 2^{g(H)}$ would require that $g_a \succeq g_{a'}$ and $g_{a'} \succeq g_a$ for it to be the case that $g_a \sim g_{a'}$, and this is in turn what is required for substitutability to exist between a and a' by definition 23, that $g_a \not\succeq g_{a'}$ is the case precludes a and a' being substitutable. Further, we can conclude therefore that $g_a \not\sim g_{a'}$ since we would require that $g_a \succeq g_{a'}$ and $g_{a'} \succeq g_a$ for it to be the case that $g_a \sim g_{a'}$ and in fact we have $g_a \not\succeq g_{a'}$, and therefore by definition 24 a is not-substitutable for a'. Since a and a' were picked arbitrarily this is true of any such a and a'.

(a cannot be selected): Note that by equation 3.7 we would require $g_a \succ g_{a'} \forall a' \in B$ in order for it to be the case that $a = a^*$. The conventional interpretation of the pre-ordering $\succeq \circ 2^{g(H)}$ would require therefore that $g_a \succeq g_{a'}$ and $g_{a'} \not\succeq g_a$ for all $a' \in B$. But note that by supposition there is some $a' \in$

B which *is* selected by the decision rule $f_K(\cdot) \subset g(H')$, so by definition 20 $\exists a' \in B : g_a \not\succeq g_{a'}$, which contradicts the requirement above for it to be the case that $a = a^*$.

Proof of theorem 10: If possible, needs can't not be met

Proof. Suppose, by way of contradiction, that there exists in the chain of implications g_a of a course of action $a \in B$ a relation $\neg\psi_s$ indicating the non-satiation of a need elicited by the environment, $\psi \in H'$, and another course of action $a' \in B$ for which a relation ψ_s exists in the chain of implications $g_{a'}$ indicating its satiation. That is

$$\exists R_{h\psi} = \neg\psi_s \in g_a \tag{8.24}$$

and

$$\exists a' \in B : \left\{ \exists R_{h\psi} = \psi_s \in g_{a'} \right\} \tag{8.25}$$

since by definitions 11 and 9 $B \subset 2^{A'} \subset 2^A$, and by definition 7 $g(H') \subset g$ (H) we have therefore that

$$\exists a' \in 2^A : \left\{ \exists R_{h\psi} = \psi_s \in g_{a'} \right\} \tag{8.26}$$

Now by definition 25 we have that

$$\exists R_{h\psi} = \neg\psi_s \in g_a \Rightarrow g_{a'} \succ g_a \, \forall a' \in 2^A : \left\{ \exists R_{h\psi} = \psi_s \in g_{a'} \right\} \tag{8.27}$$

and so we can conclude that $g_{a'} \succ g_a$. Further, we know that $a' \in B$ by supposition, and so

$$\exists a' \in B : g_{a'} \succ g_a$$

and therefore by theorem 2, $a \neq a^* : a = \{a \in B : g_a \succ g_{a'} \forall a' \in B\}$.

Proof of corollary 4: If needs can't be met, they aren't

Proof. Take a course of action $a \in B$ for which a relation exists $\neg\psi_s \in g_H(H')$ in the chain of implications g_a indicating the non-satiation of a need elicited by the environment, $\psi \in H'$. That is

$$\exists R_{h\psi} = \neg\psi_s \in g_a \tag{8.28}$$

By definition 25 therefore,

$$g_{a'} \succ g_a \, \forall a' \in 2^A : \left\{ \exists R_{h\psi} = \psi_s \in g_{a'} \right\} \tag{8.29}$$

But by supposition, if there is no action $a' \in 2^A$ so defined within B,

$$\nexists a' \in B : \left\{ \exists R_{h\psi} = \psi_s \in g_{a'} \right\} \tag{8.30}$$

Now, provided we have that g_a is strictly preferred to all other alternatives not so defined within B,

$$g_a \succ g_{a'} \, \forall a' \in B : \neg \left\{ \exists R_{h\psi} = \psi_s \in g_{a'} \right\} \tag{8.31}$$

we can conclude that because g_a is strictly preferred to all $g_{a'}$ in

$$a' \in B : \neg \left\{ \exists R_{h\psi} = \psi_s \in g_{a'} \right\} \tag{8.32}$$

and the complement in B of this set,

$$a' \in B : \left\{ \exists R_{h\psi} = \psi_s \in g_{a'} \right\} \tag{8.33}$$

is empty, we must have that

$$g_a \succ g_{a'} \, \forall a' \in B \tag{8.34}$$

And since by supposition $a \in B$, we have with theorem 2 that $a = a^* : a = \{a \in B : g_a \succ g_{a'} \forall a' \in B\}$.

Proof of theorem 11: A hierarchy of needs may enable choice between competing needs

Proof. Take that feasible action $a \in B$ which satisfies all elicited needs as can be indexed by $n \leq \bar{n}$, where $\bar{n}$ is the greatest out of all feasible actions $a' \in B$. If, as we suppose, this is the only action which so satisfies all elicited needs as can be indexed by $n \leq \bar{n}$, then by the assumption that $\bar{n}$ is the greatest out of all feasible acts $a' \in B$ there exists some $n' \leq \bar{n}$ for every $a' \in B$ such that a' does not satisfy the need as can indexed by n'. That is $\exists n' \leq \bar{n} : \neg \psi_s^n \in g_{a'} \, \forall a' \in B$. If a hierarchy of needs exists, then we may establish therefore that

$$g_a \succ g_{a'} \, \forall a' \in B \tag{8.35}$$

Since $a \in B$, we have that $a = a^*$ by definition 3.7.

Proof of theorem 12: Presence of complements may be decisive

Proof. What we wish to show is that if $a \in B : a \supset \alpha, \alpha'$, then $a = a^*$. That is, using equation 3.7, we wish to demonstrate that if $a \in B : a \supset \alpha, \alpha'$, we have that $g_a \succ g_{a''} \forall a'' \in B$, where the set $a'' \in B$ includes a'. Initially we have that this is not the case, for by supposition we have $g_{a'} \succ g_a$ when $a \not\supset \alpha'$. However, by assumption, if the complementarity between α and α' is such as we have supposed then if $a \supset \alpha, \alpha'$, we have $g_{a \supset \alpha, \alpha'} \succ g_{a'}$. We also supposed that $\succeq \circ 2^{g(H')}$ remains transitive for the preference comparison of implications of a, a' and any particular a'' and that $g_{a'} \succ g_{a''} \forall a'' \in B$. So, if $g_{a \supset \alpha, \alpha'} \succ g_{a'}$ and $g_{a'} \succ g_{a''} \forall a'' \in B$ we can therefore establish that

$$g_{a \supset \alpha, \alpha'} \succ g_{a''} \forall a'' \in B \tag{8.36}$$

where the set $a'' \in B$ includes a'. If $a \in B : a \supset \alpha, \alpha'$ then, we would have by equation 3.7 that such $a = a^*$.

Proof of theorem 13: Behaviour may be context-contingent

Proof. (Sufficiency): There has been a change in environment $v_N \rightarrow v'_N$ sufficient to induce

$$g\left(\rho\left(v'_N\right) \backslash \{R_{hh'}\}\right) : g'_{a'} \succ g'_{a''} \forall a'' \in B' \tag{8.37}$$

We have that $g'_{a'} \succ g'_{a''} \forall a'' \in B'$, and we have already by assumption that $a' \in B'$. So $a' \in B' \& g'_{a'} \succ g'_{a''} \forall a'' \in B'$ and therefore satisfies 3.7, so $a' = \{a \in B' : g'_{a'} \succ g'_{a''} \forall a'' \in B'\}$, and there will be a change of behaviour $a^* \rightarrow a'$.

(Necessity): If it is to be the case that $a' = \{a \in B' : g'_{a'} \succ g'_{a''} \forall a'' \in B'\}$ and a change of behaviour $a^* \rightarrow a'$ when $a^*, a' \in B'$, it must be the case that $g'_{a'} \succ g'_{a''} \forall a'' \in B'$ where hitherto $g_a \succ g_{a''} \forall a'' \in B$. Hence there must have been a change in the environment $v_N \rightarrow v'_N$ which, when perceived, $\rho\left(v'_N\right)$, generates an understanding $g\left(\rho\left(v'_N\right) \backslash \{R_{hh'}\}\right)$ sufficient for the implications $g'_{a'}$ to be established as more preferable than the implications $g'_{a''}$ of any other alternative $a'' \in B'$. That is, there must have been a change of the environment sufficient to induce

$$g\left(\rho\left(v'_N\right) \backslash \{R_{hh'}\}\right) : g'_{a'} \succ g'_{a''} \forall a'' \in B' \tag{8.38}$$

Proof of theorem 14: Testing for context-contingency of perception

Proof. By definition 28, sensitivity to salient information exists if for information in a particular environment $v' \subset v_N$ we can establish that

$$\rho(v') \neq \rho(v' \subset v_N) \tag{8.39}$$

Now, suppose we have two particular environments v_N and v'_N such that $v' \subset v_N$ and $v' \subset v'_N$ and

$$\rho(v' \subset v_N) \neq \rho(v' \subset v'_N) \tag{8.40}$$

If $\rho(v' \subset v_N) \neq \rho(v' \subset v'_N)$ then we know that $\exists h \lor R_{hh'} \in \rho(v' \subset v'_N)$: $h \lor R_{hh'} \notin \rho(v' \subset v_N)$. Pick without loss of generality h which satisfies this condition. By definition 6 we have that $\rho(v' \subset v'_N) = \rho(v') \cap \rho(v'_N) \subset \rho(v')$. So if we know that $h \in \rho(v' \subset v'_N)$ we therefore know that $h \in \rho(v')$. But we know that $h \notin \rho(v' \subset v_N)$. So we know that $\exists h \in \rho(v')$: $h \notin \rho(v' \subset v_N)$ and therefore that

$$\rho(v') \neq \rho(v' \subset v_N) \tag{8.41}$$

Which is the definition of context-contingence of perception. Therefore we know that there is sensitivity to salient information if we can find two particular environments v_N and v'_N such that $v' \subset v_N$ and $v' \subset v'_N$ and $\rho(v' \subset v_N) \neq \rho(v' \subset v'_N)$.

Proof of theorem 15: Salience leads to context-contingency of perception

Proof. Take some v' : $h = \rho(v')$. If

$$h \in \rho(v' \subset v_N) \Leftrightarrow \sigma(v') - \sigma(v_N) \geq \bar{\sigma} \tag{8.42}$$

for the particular environment v_N : $v' \subset v_N$, we have two possibilities with respect to the environment v_N which contains v'. Either $\sigma(v_N) \leq \sigma(v') - \bar{\sigma}$ which implies that $\sigma(v') - \sigma(v_N) \geq \bar{\sigma}$ and so $h \in \rho(v' \subset v_N)$. Or, we have that $\sigma(v_N) > \sigma(v') - \bar{\sigma}$ which implies that $\sigma(v') - \sigma(v_N) < \bar{\sigma}$ and $h \notin \rho(v' \subset v_N)$. The latter possibility is indeed a case by assumption that $\exists v_N \subset V_N : \sigma(v_N) > \sigma(v') - \bar{\sigma}$, and so there is a particular environment v_N such that $h \notin \rho(v' \subset v_N)$. But $h = \rho(v')$. By definition 6 $\rho(v' \subset v_N) = \rho(v') \cap \rho(v_N)$, so this is indeed possible, for while $h = \rho(v')$ it can, and indeed will be the case that $h \notin \rho\ (v_N)$. So we have $h \in \rho\ (v')$ (actually, $h = \rho\ (v')$), but we have $h \notin \rho\ (v' \subset v_N)$, and so we can conclude that

$$\rho(v') \neq \rho(v' \subset v_N) \tag{8.43}$$

which, by definition 28 means $\rho\ (\cdot)$ is context-contingent.

Proof of theorem 16: Percepts elicited by chains of thought

Proof. Suppose that $h_0 \in \rho\ (v_N)$. Since by assumption $s\left(R_{h_0 h_1}\right) - \sigma(v) \geq \bar{s}$, by definition 29 we have that $h_1 \in \rho\ (v_N)$. Since $h_0, h_1 \in H'$ therefore, by definition 7 $R_{h_0 h_1} \in g(H')$. Repeating the argument now for h_1, since $h_1 \in \rho\ (v_N)$ and $s(R_{h_1 h_2}) - \sigma(v_N) \geq \bar{s}$, we have by definition that $h_2 \in \rho\ (v_N)$ and so since $h_1, h_2 \in H'$ by definition 7 $R_{h_1 h_2} \in g(H')$. We may repeat this argument until we find that $R_{h_K h_{K+1}} \in g(H')$ after finding that $R_{h_k h_{k+1}} \in g(H') \forall k \in [0, K-1]$. Since therefore we have that $R_{h_k h_{k+1}} \in g(H') \forall k \in [0, K]$, we have that $R_{hh'} \in g(H') \forall R_{hh'} \in g$ and therefore $g \subset g(H')$.

Proof of theorem 17: Psychological anchors may change behaviour

Proof. By supposition, where we have v, $g(\rho\ (v_N) \backslash \{R_{hh'}\})$ causes it to be the case that $g_{a'} \succ g_a$. Since we supposed that $g_{a''} \succeq g_a \vee g_{a'}$ or $g_{a''} \preceq g_a \vee g_{a'}$ or some mixture for all $a'' \in B$, our assumption that $g_{a''} \not\succeq g_a \vee g_{a'} \forall a'' \in B$ implies that $g_{a'} \succ g_a \& g_{a''} \forall a'' \in B$. Therefore, since we supposed a and a' remain feasible, by definition (equation 3.7), we have that $a' = a^*$ when we have v_N and $\rho(v_N) \not\supset \bar{\delta}$.

Now take v'_N and repeat the argument. Here we have that $g(\rho(v'_N) \backslash \{R'_{hh'}\}) = g(H' \cup \bar{\delta})$ causes it to be the case that $g_a \succ g_{a'}$. Since we supposed that $g_{a''} \succeq g_a \vee g_{a'}$ or $g_{a''} \preceq g_a \vee g_{a'}$ or some mixture for all $a'' \in B$, our assumption that $g_{a''} \not\succeq g_a \vee g_{a'} \forall a'' \in B$ implies that $g_a \succ g_{a'} \& g_{a''} \forall a'' \in B$. Therefore, since we supposed a and a' remain feasible, by definition (equation 3.7), we have that $a = a^*$ when we have v'_N and $\rho(v'_N) \supset \bar{\delta}$.

Thus the movement $v_N \rightarrow v'_N$ between environments causes the movement between actions $a' \rightarrow a$, which is to say that the introduction into perception of the anchor $\rho(v_N) \not\supset \bar{\delta} \rightarrow \rho(v'_N) \supset \bar{\delta}$ causes a change of behaviour $a' = a^* \rightarrow a = a^*$.

Proof of theorem 18: Cognitive dissonance implies hypothesis filtering and preference for confirmation

Proof. *(Hypothesis filtering)*: Take the law of resistance to dissonance, which is that

$$\frac{\partial p(R_{hh'} \in g(H))}{\partial |\{R_{h''h'''} \in g(H') : R_{hh'} \Rightarrow \neg R_{h''h'''}\}|} \leq 0 \tag{8.44}$$

Suppose we take an apparent relation $R_{hh'} \in \rho (v_N)$ which is neutral, which does not contradict any other relation $R_{h''h'''} \in g(H')$ that is

$$R_{hh'} \not\Rightarrow R_{h''h'''} \vee \neg R_{h''h'''} \forall R_{h''h'''} \in g(H) \tag{8.45}$$

So $|\{R_{h''h'''} \in g(H') : R_{hh'} \Rightarrow \neg R_{h''h'''}\}| = 0$.

Suppose now that there is some relation $R_{h''h'''} \in g(H')$ which $R_{hh'}$ contradicts. That is $\exists R_{h''h'''} \in g(H') : R_{hh'} \Rightarrow \neg R_{h''h'''}$ and thus $|\{R_{h''h'''} \in g(H') : R_{hh'} \Rightarrow \neg R_{h''h'''}\}| > 0$. And therefore

$$\partial |\{R_{h''h'''} \in g(H') : R_{hh'} \Rightarrow \neg R_{h''h'''}\}| > 0 \tag{8.46}$$

By the law of resistance to dissonance then

$$\partial p(R_{hh'} \in g(H)) \leq 0 \tag{8.47}$$

and we can conclude that an individual is less likely to accept any relations $R_{hh'} \in \rho (v_N)$ which contradict relations contained within $g(H')$, where $H' \subset \rho (v_N)$, than those which do not. That is, an individual is more likely to reject any relations $R_{hh'} \in \rho (v_N)$ which contradict relations contained within $g(H')$, where $H' \subset \rho (v_{N(g)})$, than those which do not, and hypothesis filtering exists in the environment v_N.

(Confirmation bias): Again, take the law of resistance to dissonance

$$\frac{\partial p(R_{hh'} \in g(H))}{\partial |\{R_{h''h'''} \in g(H') : R_{hh'} \Rightarrow \neg R_{h''h'''}\}|} \leq 0 \tag{8.48}$$

Suppose we take an apparent relation $R_{hh'} \in \rho (v_N)$ which contradicts some relations $R_{h''h'''} \in g(H')$, that is $|\{R_{h''h'''} \in g(H') : R_{hh'} \Rightarrow \neg R_{h''h'''}\}| > 0$. Now suppose that there exist no relations $R_{h''h'''} \in g(H')$ which $R_{hh'} \in \rho (v_N)$ contradicts, that is $\nexists R_{h''h'''} \in g(H') : R_{hh'} \Rightarrow \neg R_{h''h'''}$, so that we have $|\{R_{h''h'''} \in g(H') : R_{hh'} \Rightarrow \neg R_{h''h'''}\}| = 0$. Therefore

$$\partial |\{R_{h''h'''} \in g(H') : R_{hh'} \Rightarrow \neg R_{h''h'''}\}| < 0 \tag{8.49}$$

By the law of dissonance

$$\partial p(R_{hh'} \in g(H)) \geq 0 \tag{8.50}$$

and we can conclude an individual is more likely to accept any relations $R_{hh'} \in \rho\ (v_N)$ which do not contradict relations contained within $g(H')$, where $H' \subset \rho\ (v_N)$, than those which do, and preference for confirmation exists in the environment v_N.

Proof of theorem 19: When ideas are "made to stick"

Proof. It will be advantageous, first, to establish the response of the likelihood $p(\{R_{hh'}\}^P \subset g(H))$ of any proposed idea $\{R_{hh'}\}^P$ being incorporated into the mind of the individual, to the likelihood $p(R_{hh'} \in g(H))$ of any individual relation $R_{hh'} \in \{R_{hh'}\}^P$ within it being incorporated into the mind of the individual. Note that because the event $\{R_{hh'}\}^P \subset g(H)$ is contingent upon every single relation $R_{hh'} \in \{R_{hh'}\}^P$ being incorporated into $g(H)$, if there is a single relation $R_{hh'} \in \{R_{hh'}\}^P$ such that $R_{hh'} \notin g(H)$ then $\{R_{hh'}\}^P \not\subset g(H)$. That is,

$$\exists R_{hh'} \in \{R_{hh'}\}^P : R_{hh'} \notin g(H) \Rightarrow \{R_{hh'}\}^P \not\subset g(H) \tag{8.51}$$

Let us now prove each of the five properties 1–5 in turn.

1. Take the idea $\{R_{hh'}\}^P$ and add a new relation $R_{h''h'''}$ to be included within that idea. By condition 8.51, whether $R_{h''h'''}$ is incorporated into $g(H)$ will determine whether or not $\{R_{hh'}\}^P \subset g(H)$. Now because of this contingency upon every one of the individual links, we can establish a relation between the likelihood $p(R_{h''h'''} \cup \{R_{hh'}\}^P \subset g(H))$ of the expanded idea $R_{h''h'''} \cup \{R_{hh'}\}^P$ being incorporated into $g(H)$ and the likelihood $p(\{R_{hh'}\}^P \subset g(H))$ of the original idea $\{R_{hh'}\}^P$ being incorporated into $g(H)$. We have two possibilities, either

$$p(R_{h''h'''} \in g(H)) \geq p\big(\{R_{hh'}\}^P \subset g(H)\big) \tag{8.52}$$

where $p(R_{h''h'''} \in g(H))$ and $p(\{R_{hh'}\}^P \subset g(H))$ are conditioned on whatever events they are conditioned on. The likelihood $p(R_{h''h'''} \cup \{R_{hh'}\}^P \subset g(H))$ is limited by $p(\{R_{hh'}\}^P \subset g(H))$ since condition 8.51 requires *all* $R_{hh'} \in \{R_{hh'}\}^P$ to be incorporated, and so the likelihood $p(R_{h''h'''} \cup \{R_{hh'}\}^P \subset$

$g(H)$) is equal to the original likelihood $p(\{R_{hh'}\}^P \subset g(H))$. So

$$p(R_{h''h'''} \in g(H)) \geq p(\{R_{hh'}\}^P \subset g(H))$$
$$\Rightarrow p(R_{h''h'''} \cup \{R_{hh'}\}^P \subset g(H)) = p(\{R_{hh'}\}^P \subset g(H)) \tag{8.53}$$

Or, alternatively we have

$$p(R_{h''h'''} \in g(H)) < p(\{R_{hh'}\}^P \subset g(H)) \tag{8.54}$$

where $p(R_{h''h'''} \in g(H))$ is conditioned on whatever events it is conditioned on, and so the likelihood $p(R_{h''h'''} \cup \{R_{hh'}\}^P \subset g(H))$ is less than the original likelihood $p(\{R_{hh'}\}^P \subset g(H))$, because of the contingency 8.51. So

$$p(R_{h''h'''} \in g(H)) < p(\{R_{hh'}\}^P \subset g(H))$$
$$\Rightarrow p(R_{h''h'''} \cup \{R_{hh'}\}^P \subset g(H)) < p(\{R_{hh'}\}^P \subset g(H)) \tag{8.55}$$

The relations 8.53 and 8.55 therefore imply that with the addition of new relations to the idea, $R_{h''h'''} \cup \{R_{hh'}\}^P$, we have $\partial p(\{R_{hh'}\}^P \subset g(H)) \leq 0$. Therefore, we have that

$$\frac{\partial p(\{R_{hh'}\}^P \subset g(H))}{\partial |\{R_{hh'}\}^P|} \leq 0 \tag{8.56}$$

This proves property 1.

2. Let us now take an individual relation $R_{h''h'''} \in \{R_{hh'}\}^P$ which is already incorporated within $g(H)$. By definition 13

$$R_{h''h'''} \in g(H) \Rightarrow p(R_{h''h'''} \in g(H)) = 1 \tag{8.57}$$

Since by definition 13 $p(R_{h''h'''} \in g(H)) \in [0, 1]$ then, as we move between the states $R_{h''h'''} \notin g(H)$ and $R_{h''h'''} \in g(H)$ we find $p(R_{h''h'''} \in g(H)) \to 1$. Now, again because of condition 8.51,

$$\exists R_{hh'} \in \{R_{hh'}\}^P : R_{hh'} \notin g(H) \Rightarrow p(\{R_{hh'}\}^P \not\subset g(H)) \tag{8.58}$$

we know that the event $\{R_{hh'}\}^P \subset g(H)$ is contingent upon the incorporation of all individual relations $R_{hh'} \in \{R_{hh'}\}^P$ being incorporated. With respect to the likelihood of the event $\{R_{hh'}\}^P \subset g(H)$ we therefore have two possibilities as we move between the states $R_{h''h'''} \notin g(H)$ and $R_{h''h'''} \in g(H)$. Either

$$p(R_{h''h'''} \in g(H)) > \{R_{hh'}\}^P \subset g(H) \tag{8.59}$$

and so the movement $p(R_{h''h'''} \in g(H)) \to 1$ has no effect upon

$p(\{R_{hh'}\}^P \subset g(H))$ since it was not, by condition 8.51, the limiting factor on $p(\{R_{hh'}\}^P \subset g(H))$, and

$$p(R_{h''h'''} \in g(H)) \quad \to 1 \Rightarrow \partial p(\{R_{hh'}\}^P \subset g(H)) = 0 \qquad (8.60)$$

Or, alternatively, we have that $p(R_{h''h'''} \in g(H))$ *was* the limiting factor on $p(\{R_{hh'}\}^P \subset g(H))$ by condition 8.51, so

$$p(R_{h''h'''} \in g(H)) = p(\{R_{hh'}\}^P \subset g(H)) \qquad (8.61)$$

and so the movement $p(R_{h''h'''} \in g(H)) \to 1$ has at least no effect upon $p(\{R_{hh'}\}^P \subset g(H))$, and

$$p(R_{h''h'''} \in g(H)) \quad \to 1 \Rightarrow \partial p(\{R_{hh'}\}^P \subset g(H)) \geq 0 \qquad (8.62)$$

So we can conclude from relations 8.60 and 8.62 that as we find individual relations $R_{hh'} \in \{R_{hh'}\}^P$ already incorporated into $g(H)$ we have $\partial p (\{R_{hh'}\}^P \subset g(H)) \geq 0$. Therefore we have that

$$\frac{\partial p(\{R_{hh'}\}^P \subset g(H))}{\partial |R_{hh'} \in \{R_{hh'}\}^P : R_{hh'} \in g(H)|} \geq 0 \qquad (8.63)$$

This proves 2.

Before proving properties 3–5, let us derive the relation between the likelihood of the idea $\{R_{hh'}\}^P$ being incorporated into $g(H)$, $p(\{R_{hh'}\}^P \subset g(H))$ and the likelihood of the individual relation $R_{hh'}$ being incorporated into $g(H)$, $p(R_{hh'} \in g(H))$. Note again that because of condition 8.51

$$\exists R_{hh'} \in \{R_{hh'}\}^P : R_{hh'} \notin g(H) \Rightarrow \{R_{hh'}\}^P \not\subset g(H) \qquad (8.64)$$

it is the case that an increase in the likelihood of any one connection *not* being incorporated *at least* has no effect on the likelihood $p(\{R_{hh'}\}^P \subset g(H))$ of the idea as a whole being incorporated, and thus causes $p(\{R_{hh'}\}^P \not\subset g(H))$ to vary in proportion with it

$$p(\{R_{hh'}\}^P \not\subset g(H)) \propto p(R_{hh'} \notin g(H)) \qquad (8.65)$$

Which allows us to conclude that

$$\frac{\partial p(\{R_{hh'}\}^P \not\subset g(H))}{\partial p(R_{hh'} \notin g(H))} \geq 0 \qquad (8.66)$$

Now, the law of complements tells us that

$$p\big(\{R_{hh'}\}^P \not\subset g(H)\big) = 1 - p\big(\{R_{hh'}\}^P \subset g(H)\big) \tag{8.67}$$

$$p(R_{hh'} \not\in g(H)) = 1 - p(R_{hh'} \in g(H)) \tag{8.68}$$

Now substituting this into equation 8.66 we have that

$$\frac{\partial\big[1 - p(\{R_{hh'}\}^P \subset g(H))\big]}{\partial[1 - p(R_{hh'} \in g(H))]} \geq 0 \tag{8.69}$$

Applying some tautologies, we get that

$$\frac{\partial[1 - p(\{R_{hh'}\}^P \subset g(H))]}{\partial p(\{R_{hh'}\}^P \subset g(H))}\frac{\partial p(\{R_{hh'}\}^P \subset g(H))}{\partial p(R_{hh'} \in g(H))}\frac{\partial p(R_{hh'} \in g(H))}{\partial[1 - p(R_{hh'} \in g(H))]}$$
$$\geq 0 \tag{8.70}$$

It is fairly obvious that

$$\frac{\partial\big[1 - p(\{R_{hh'}\}^P \subset g(H))\big]}{\partial p\big(\{R_{hh'}\}^P \subset g(H)\big)} < 0 \tag{8.71}$$

and

$$\frac{\partial p(R_{hh'} \in g(H))}{\partial[1 - p(R_{hh'} \in g(H))]} < 0 \tag{8.72}$$

and so by equation 8.70 it must be the case that

$$\frac{\partial p\big(\{R_{hh'}\}^P \subset g(H)\big)}{\partial p(R_{hh'} \in g(H))} \geq 0 \,\forall R_{hh'} \in \{R_{hh'}\}^P \tag{8.73}$$

This makes the process of proving properties 3–5 substantially easier. If we can establish that either $\partial p(R_{hh'} \in g(H)) \geq 0$ or $\partial p(R_{hh'} \in g(H)) \leq 0$ then we will know by equation 8.73 therefore that $\partial p(\{R_{hh'}\}^P \subset g(H)) \geq 0$ or $\partial p(\{R_{hh'}\}^P \subset g(H)) \leq 0$ respectively. Let us turn to each property in turn:

3. Note that by the law of suggestion (definition 14), we have

$$\frac{\partial p(R_{hh'} \in g(H))}{\partial I(R_{hh'} \in \rho(v_N))} \geq 0 \tag{8.74}$$

where

$$I(R_{hh'} \in \rho(v_N)) = \begin{cases} 1 & \text{if } R_{hh'} \in \rho(v_N) \\ 0 & \text{if } R_{hh'} \notin \rho(v_N) \end{cases} \qquad (8.75)$$

Multiplying this by equation 8.73 we have

$$\frac{\partial p(\{R_{hh'}\}^P \subset g(H))}{\partial p(R_{hh'} \in g(H))} \frac{\partial p(R_{hh'} \in g(H))}{\partial I(R_{hh'} \in \rho(v_N))} \geq 0 \,\forall\, R_{hh'} \in \{R_{hh'}\}^P \qquad (8.76)$$

and

$$\frac{\partial p(\{R_{hh'}\}^P \subset g(H))}{\partial I(R_{hh'} \in \rho(v_N))} \geq 0 \,\forall\, R_{hh'} \in \{R_{hh'}\}^P \qquad (8.77)$$

But notice that, by definition 5, a relation $R_{hh'}$ may be perceived, $R_{hh'} \in \rho(v_N)$, only if the objects of reality it relates h,h' are also perceived

$$R_{hh'} \in \rho(v_N) \Rightarrow h, h' \in \rho(v_N) \qquad (8.78)$$

and so from the negation (without loss of generality) $h \notin \rho(v_N)$ of this necessary condition we may infer that $R_{hh'} \notin \rho(v_N)$

$$h \notin \rho(v_N) \Rightarrow R_{hh'} \notin \rho(v_N) \qquad (8.79)$$

Now imagine there is an indicator function

$$I_h(h \in \rho(v_N)) = \begin{cases} 1 & \text{if } h \in \rho(v_N) \\ 0 & \text{if } h' \notin \rho(v_N) \end{cases} \qquad (8.80)$$

The implication 8.79 tells us that if $I_h(h \in \rho(v_N)) = 0$ then $I(R_{hh'} \in \rho(v_N)) = 0$, but if $I_h(h \in \rho(v_N)) = 1$ then $I(R_{hh'} \in \rho(v_N)) \geq 0$ so

$$\frac{\partial I(R_{hh'} \in \rho(v_N))}{\partial I_h(h \in \rho(v_N))} \geq 0 \qquad (8.81)$$

Multiply this now by equation 8.77 and we get

$$\frac{\partial p(\{R_{hh'}\}^P \subset g(H))}{\partial I(R_{hh'} \in \rho(v_N))} \frac{\partial I(R_{hh'} \in \rho(v_N))}{\partial I_h(h \in \rho(v_N))} \geq 0 \,\forall\, R_{hh'} \in \{R_{hh'}\}^P \qquad (8.82)$$

and

$$\frac{\partial p\left(\{R_{hh'}\}^{P} \subset g(H)\right)}{\partial I_h(h \in \rho(v_N))} \geq 0 \,\forall R_{hh'} \in \{R_{hh'}\}^{P} \tag{8.83}$$

However, notice that if, as we assume, individual i's perception, $\rho\ (\cdot)$, has the salience property 6.4, then

$$h \in \rho(v' \subset v_N) \Leftrightarrow \sigma(v') - \sigma(v_N) \geq \bar{\sigma} \tag{8.84}$$

where $v' \in 2^{v_N} : h = \rho(v')$. So if $\sigma(v') - \sigma(v_N) \geq \bar{\sigma}$ then $h \in \rho\ (v' \subset v_N)$ and (by equation 8.80) $I_h(h \in \rho\ (v_N)) = 1$, and if $\sigma(v') - \sigma(v_N) < \bar{\sigma}$ then $h \notin \rho\ (v' \subset v_N)$ and (by equation 8.80) $I_h(h \in \rho\ (v_N)) = 0$, so we have

$$\frac{\partial I_h(h \in \rho(v_N))}{\partial[\sigma(v') - \sigma(v_N)]} \geq 0 \tag{8.85}$$

where $v' \in 2^{v_N} : h = \rho(v')$. Now if we multiply 8.85 by 8.83 we get

$$\frac{\partial p(\{R_{hh'}\}^{P} \subset g(H))}{\partial I_h(h \in \rho(v_N))} \frac{\partial I_h(h \in \rho(v_N))}{\partial[\sigma(v') - \sigma(v_N)]} \geq 0 \,\forall v' \in 2^{v_N} : h$$

$$= \rho(v') \,\& R_{hh'} \in \{R_{hh'}\}^{P} \tag{8.86}$$

and so

$$\frac{\partial p\left(\{R_{hh'}\}^{P} \subset g(H)\right)}{\partial[\sigma(v') - \sigma(v_N)]} \geq 0 \,\forall v' \in 2^{v_N} : h = \rho(v') \,\& R_{hh'} \in \{R_{hh'}\}^{P} \tag{8.87}$$

4. By the law of resistance to dissonance (definition 16) we have that

$$\frac{\partial p(R_{hh'} \in g(H))}{\partial|\{R_{h''h'''} \in g(H') : R_{hh'} \Rightarrow \neg R_{h''h'''}\}|} \geq 0 \,\forall R_{hh'} \in \{R_{hh'}\}^{P} \tag{8.88}$$

Multiplying this by equation 8.73 we have

$$\frac{\partial p(\{R_{hh'}\}^{P} \subset g(H))}{\partial p(R_{hh'} \in g(H))} \frac{\partial p(R_{hh'} \in g(H))}{\partial|\{R_{h''h'''} \in g(H') : R_{hh'} \Rightarrow \neg R_{h''h'''}\}|} \geq 0 \,\forall R_{hh'}$$

$$\in \{R_{hh'}\}P \tag{8.89}$$

and so

$$\frac{\partial p(\{R_{hh'}\}^{P} \subset g(H))}{\partial|\{R_{h''h'''} \in g(H') : R_{hh'} \Rightarrow \neg R_{h''h'''}\}|} \geq 0 \,\forall R_{hh'} \in \{R_{hh'}\}^{P} \tag{8.90}$$

5. By the law of resistance to changes at the core of personal constructs (definition 15) we have that

$$\frac{\partial p(R_{hh'} \in g(H))}{\partial c(C_{g_H(H)}(h) \quad C_{g_H(H)}(h'))} \geq 0 \,\forall\, R_{hh'} \in \{R_{hh'}\}^P \tag{8.91}$$

Multiplying this by equation 8.73 we have

$$\frac{\partial p(\{R_{hh'}\}^P \subset g(H))}{\partial p(R_{hh'} \in g(H))} \frac{\partial p(R_{hh'} \in g(H))}{\partial c\left(C_{g(H)}(h) \quad C_{g(H)}(h')\right)} \geq 0 \,\forall\, R_{hh'}$$

$$\in \{R_{hh'}\}^P \tag{8.92}$$

and so

$$\frac{\partial p(\{R_{hh'}\}^P \subset g(H))}{\partial c\left(C_{g(H)}(h) \quad C_{g(H)}(h')\right)} \geq 0 \,\forall\, R_{hh'} \in \{R_{hh'}\}^P \tag{8.93}$$

Index

action, definition of 21–23
aesthetics 26–27, 49–53, 73, 81
Akerlof, G. 37, 90
akrasia 71
Amadae, S. 37
analysis: definition of 18; process of
17–20, 22, 36, 41, 43, 79, 85, 89
anchors / anchoring 50, 80–84;
non-inert, definition of 81
Archer, M. 40, 48
archetypes, Jungian 52, 83
Ariely, D. 82
Aristotle 74, 78; *Rhetoric* 61
Artificial Intelligence 5, 37
availability heuristic 78–79
axes, personal construct theory 51, 79, 82
Ayer, A. J. 42
Ayres, C. 49

Bauermeister, R. 71
Becker, G. 70
behaviour: context contingency 69–70;
definition of 21–22; theory of
23–28
behavioural drives, motivation 50–51,
53, 83
behavioural economics 69–70, 85
Bennett, M. 4
Bergson, H. 86
bisociation 8, 31
Boulding, K. 7, 19
Bourdieu, P. 48
Briggs Myers, I. 28
Buridan's ass 30
Burke, E. 26

Cambridge Social Ontology 49
Campbell, J. 52
Chalmers, D. 4
classification, mind as system of 7,
18–19, 42, 77
Coase, R. 48
cognitive dissonance 34–35, 86–90,
88–89
cognitive theory, psychology 42–46,
50, 61, 77
Commons, J. R. 49
complementarity 65–66; definition of 65
complexes, psychological 50–51
computer / computational, mind as
43, 53
confirmation, preference for 86
consciousness 4–6, 8–10, 15, 26, 28,
45–47, 52; definition of 4, 10
core, of mental networks, centrality
in 34–35, 37, 50, 52–53, 58, 90
creativity 8–9, 31–33, 35
culture 48

Debreu, G. 40, 53
decay, of mental networks 35–36,
71, 105
de Certeau, M. 48
decision, theory of 27–28
default, preference for 84
Dennett, D. 5
Descartes, R. 3–4, 36
developmental psychology 32
Dewey, J. 7, 32, 45
Dopfer, K. 46, 48
Drakopoulos, S. 58

124   *Index*

For Product Safety Concerns and Information please contact our EU
representative GPSR@taylorandfrancis.com
Taylor & Francis Verlag GmbH, Kaufingerstraße 24, 80331 München, Germany

www.ingramcontent.com/pod-product-compliance
Ingram Content Group UK Ltd.
Pitfield, Milton Keynes, MK11 3LW, UK
UKHW021423080625
459435UK00011B/131